New

WITHDRAWN

Y0-DLR-353

346.013 Ja
Jasper, Margaret C.
How to protect your
 challenged child

STACKS

HOW TO PROTECT YOUR CHALLENGED CHILD

by
Margaret C. Jasper

Oceana's Legal Almanac Series:
Law for the Layperson

2005
Oceana Publications, Inc.
Dobbs Ferry, New York

Information contained in this work has been obtained by Oceana Publications from sources believed to be reliable. However, neither the Publisher nor its authors guarantee the accuracy or completeness of any information published herein, and neither Oceana nor its authors shall be responsible for any errors, omissions or damages arising from the use of this information. This work is published with the understanding that Oceana and its authors are supplying information, but are not attempting to render legal or other professional services. If such services are required, the assistance of an appropriate professional should be sought.

> You may order this or any Oceana publication by visiting Oceana's website at http://www.oceanalaw.com

Library of Congress Control Number: 2005925304

ISBN 0-379-11397-X

Oceana's Legal Almanac Series: Law for the Layperson
ISSN 1075-7376

©2005 by Oceana Publications, Inc.

All rights reserved. No part of this publication may be reproduced or transmitted in any form or by any means, electronic or mechanical, including photocopy, recording, xerography, or any information storage and retrieval system, without permission in writing from the publisher.

Manufactured in the United States of America on acid-free paper.

To My Husband Chris

Your love and support
are my motivation and inspiration

-and-

In memory of my son, Jimmy

Table of Contents

ABOUT THE AUTHOR ix
INTRODUCTION xi

CHAPTER 1:
CHILD ADVOCACY

REACH OUT 1
WHAT IS AN ADVOCATE? 2
YOU ARE YOUR CHILD'S MOST EFFECTIVE ADVOCATE 2
PROTECTING YOUR CHILD FROM ABUSE 3
PREPARING YOUR CHILD FOR EMERGENCIES AND DISASTERS 4
   At Home 5
      Emergency Instructions 5
      Supplies 5
      Contacts 5
   At School 5
   Away From Home 6

CHAPTER 2:
WHAT DOES IT MEAN TO BE A CHALLENGED CHILD?

IN GENERAL 7
RATING MENTAL FUNCTIONING 7
AUTISM 8
ACQUIRED IMMUNE DEFICIENCY SYNDROME (AIDS) 8
EMOTIONAL DISTURBANCE 9
LEARNING DISABILITIES 9
MENTAL RETARDATION 10
MULTIPLE DISABILITIES 10
ORTHOPEDIC IMPAIRMENTS 10
TRAUMATIC BRAIN INJURY 10
HEARING IMPAIRMENT 11
VISUAL IMPAIRMENT 11
DEAF-BLINDNESS 11
SPEECH OR LANGUAGE IMPAIRMENTS 11

OTHER HEALTH IMPAIRMENTS 11
ATTENTION DEFICIT HYPERACTIVITY DISORDER (ADHD) 11
   Statistics. 12
   Causation. 12
   Treatment 13
   Educational Intervention. 13
HIDDEN DISABILITIES 13

CHAPTER 3:
EARLY INTERVENTION SERVICES

WHAT IS EARLY INTERVENTION? 15
ELIGIBILITY 15
THE EVALUATION PROCESS 16
ASSESSMENT. 16
THE INDIVIDUALIZED FAMILY SERVICE PLAN (IFSP) 17
COSTS 18
AGING OUT OF THE EARLY INTERVENTION PROGRAM 18
EARLY HEARING DETECTION AND INTERVENTION PROGRAM 19
   Diagnostic Testing. 19
      Auditory Brainstem Response (ABR) Test 20
      Otoacoustic Emissions (OAE) Test 20
   False Positives 20

CHAPTER 4:
YOUR CHILD'S RIGHT TO A FREE APPROPRIATE PUBLIC EDUCATION

EDUCATION LAW. 21
COMPULSORY EDUCATION 21
COMPULSORY SPECIAL EDUCATION. 22
VOCATIONAL SCHOOLS. 22
STATE EDUCATIONAL SYSTEMS 23
THE SPECIAL EDUCATION PROCESS. 23
   Child Find 23
   The IEP Meeting 24
   Consent 24
   Services 25
   Progress Reports. 25
   Annual Review 25
   Reevaluation 25
   Stay Put Provision 26
THE INDIVIDUALIZED EDUCATION PROGRAM (IEP) 26
   Current Performance 26
   Annual Goals 26
   Special Education and Related Services 26

Participation with Nondisabled Children 27
Participation in State and District Tests 27
Dates and Places of Services 27
Need for Transition Services 27
Progress 27
THE IEP TEAM MEMBERS 27
    Parents 28
    Teachers 28
    Evaluation Results Interpreter 28
    School District Representative 28
    Related Services Professionals 28
    The Student 29
RELATED SERVICES 29
RIGHT TO TRANSPORTATION 30
SPECIAL FACTORS 31
    Behavior 31
    English Proficiency 31
    Blindness or Visual Impairment 31
    Communication Needs 31
    Assistive Technology 31
PLACEMENT DECISIONS 31
ACCESS TO THE IEP 32
TRANSITION SERVICES 32
ASSISTIVE TECHNOLOGY 32
SCHOOL DISCIPLINE FOR DISABLED CHILDREN 33
    Disciplinary Removal from Regular Placement 34
    Discipline for Weapon and Drug Offenses 35

CHAPTER 5:
KEEPING YOUR CHILD'S SCHOOL RECORDS CONFIDENTIAL

IN GENERAL 37
THE FAMILY EDUCATIONAL RIGHTS AND PRIVACY ACT OF 1974 37
CONSENT 38
AMENDING EDUCATION RECORDS 38
PSYCHIATRIC RECORDS 39
SUBPOENAS 39
FEES 39
LIMITATIONS 39
THE COMPLAINT PROCEDURE 39
HEARINGS 40

CHAPTER 6:
HOME SCHOOLING YOUR CHILD

IN GENERAL 43
YOUR RIGHT TO HOME SCHOOL YOUR CHILD 43
HOME SCHOOLING YOUR CHALLENGED CHILD 43
COURSE CURRICULUM 44
EVALUATION 45
PROBATION 46
HOME SCHOOL TEACHER 46
HOME SCHOOL CALENDAR 47
MISCELLANEOUS PROVISIONS 47
   Immunizations 47
   Services and Supplies 47
   Recordkeeping 48
   Extracurricular Activities 48
COLLEGE ADMISSION 48

CHAPTER 7:
OBTAINING FINANCIAL AND HEALTH BENEFITS FOR YOUR CHILD

IN GENERAL 51
SUPPLEMENTAL SECURITY INCOME (SSI) 51
   Eligibility for SSI/SSDI 51
   Redetermination 52
   Your Right to Appeal 53
   Dedicated Accounts 54
MEDICAID 55
   The 1915 Katie Beckett Medicaid Waiver 55
   Medically Needy Programs 55
   The Early and Periodic Screening, Diagnostic, and Treatment Program (EPSDT) 56
YOUR CHILD'S EARNINGS 57
STATE CHILDREN'S HEALTH INSURANCE PROGRAM (SCHIP) 57
TITLE V OF THE SOCIAL SECURITY ACT 57
   The Integrated Services Branch 58
   The Genetics Services Branch 58

CHAPTER 8:
DISABILITY LEGISLATION

CASE LAW AND LEGISLATIVE DEVELOPMENTS 61
   Brown v. Board of Education 61
   Mills v. Board of Education of District of Columbia 61
   Board of Education v. Rowley 62

THE REHABILITATION ACT OF 1973 62
THE EDUCATION FOR ALL HANDICAPPED CHILDREN ACT OF 1975 (EAHCA) 63
THE HANDICAPPED CHILDREN'S PROTECTION ACT OF 1986 64
THE INDIVIDUALS WITH DISABILITIES EDUCATION ACT (IDEA) 64
   Part A: General Provisions, Definitions and Other Issues 64
   Part B: Assistance for Education of All Children with Disabilities 64
   Part C: Infants and Toddlers with Disabilities 64
   Part D: National Activities to Improve Education of Children with
   Disabilities 65
   Covered Persons 65
   A Free Appropriate Public Education 65
   The Individual Education Program (IEP) 65
   The IDEA Amendments of 1997 66
      Part A: General Provisions 67
      Part B: Assistance for Education of All Children with Disabilities. 67
      Part C: Infants and Toddlers with Disabilities 67
      Part D: National Activities to Improve Education of Children with
      Disabilities 67
   Significant Changes 68
      Child with a Disability 68
      Seriously Emotionally Disturbed 68
      Parent Counseling and Training 68
      Transportation 68
      Removals and Suspensions 68
      Graduation 69
      Advancement 69
      The Least Restrictive Environment 69
      Parentally Placed Children 70
      Placement 70
      Assistive Technology 70
      Extended School Year 70
      Parent Participation in Eligibility and Placement Decisions 70
      Reevaluations 70
   Private Education Under the Individuals With Disabilities Education Act. 71
THE FAMILY EDUCATIONAL RIGHTS AND PRIVACY ACT OF 1974 72
THE AMERICANS WITH DISABILITIES ACT OF 1990 73
   Disability Discrimination Under Title II of the ADA 73
THE IMPROVING AMERICA'S SCHOOLS ACT OF 1994 75
THE NO CHILD LEFT BEHIND ACT 75

CHAPTER 9:
TRANSITIONING YOUR CHILD FROM SCHOOL TO THE WORKPLACE
HELPING YOUR CHILD MAKE THE TRANSITION 79
WORK-BASED LEARNING ACTIVITIES 80

Information Interviews 81
Job Shadowing 81
Internships 81
Apprenticeship. 81
EMPLOYMENT DISCRIMINATION 81
THE NATIONAL COLLABORATIVE ON WORKFORCE AND DISABILITY 82
Preparatory Experiences....................................... 82
Work-Based Learning 83
Youth Development & Youth Leadership 83
Connecting Activities 83
ONE-STOPS.. 83
THE TICKET TO WORK PROGRAM 84
Title I... 84
Title II 85

CHAPTER 10:
PLANNING YOUR ESTATE WHEN YOU HAVE A CHALLENGED CHILD

PLANNING AHEAD.. 87
YOUR WILL 88
Name an Advisor 88
Name an Advocate 88
Name a Guardian... 88
Court-Appointed Conservator 89
TRUSTS... 89
Support Trust 89
Special Needs Trust... 90

APPENDICES
1: ADVOCACY GROUPS FOR PARENTS OF DISABLED CHILDREN........ 91
2: NATIONAL DISABILITY ORGANIZATIONS 97
3: DSM-IV CRITERIA FOR ATTENTION DEFICIT/HYPERACTIVITY
DISORDER.. 113
4: CHILD DEVELOPMENT CHECKLIST—BIRTH TO 4 YEARS OF AGE.... 117
5: DIRECTORY OF STATE SPECIAL EDUCATION AGENCIES 121
6: COMPULSORY SCHOOL ATTENDANCE, BY STATE AND AGE 129
7: COMPULSORY SPECIAL EDUCATION SERVICES FOR STUDENTS,
BY STATE AND AGE 131
8: SAMPLE INDIVIDUALIZED EDUCATION PROGRAM 133
9: SPECIAL EDUCATION INFORMATION RESOURCES 135
10: DIRECTORY OF ATTORNEYS WHO REPRESENT PARENTS OF
CHILDREN WITH DISABILITIES.................................. 137

11: SELECTED PROVISIONS OF SECTION 504 OF THE REHABILITATION ACT OF 1973 (29 U.S.C. 794) 153
12: SELECTED PROVISIONS OF THE INDIVIDUALS WITH DISABILITIES EDUCATION ACT (20 U.S.C. 33) 157
13: SELECTED PROVISIONS OF THE AMERICANS WITH DISABILITIES ACT OF 1990 201
14: TRANSITIONING RESOURCE DIRECTORY. 205
15: TABLE OF TICKETS ISSUED UNDER THE TICKET TO WORK PROGRAM AS OF MAY 2005, BY STATE 209
GLOSSARY. 211
BIBLIOGRAPHY AND ADDITIONAL RESOURCES. 223

ABOUT THE AUTHOR

MARGARET C. JASPER is an attorney engaged in the general practice of law in South Salem, New York, concentrating in the areas of personal injury and entertainment law. Ms. Jasper holds a Juris Doctor degree from Pace University School of Law, White Plains, New York, is a member of the New York and Connecticut bars, and is certified to practice before the United States District Courts for the Southern and Eastern Districts of New York, the United States Court of Appeals for the Second Circuit, and the United States Supreme Court.

Ms. Jasper has been appointed to the panel of arbitrators of the American Arbitration Association and the law guardian panel for the Family Court of the State of New York, is a member of the Association of Trial Lawyers of America, and is a New York State licensed real estate broker and member of the Westchester County Board of Realtors, operating as Jasper Real Estate, in South Salem, New York. Margaret Jasper maintains a website at http://www.JasperLawOffice.com.

Ms. Jasper is the author and general editor of the following legal almanacs: AIDS Law; The Americans with Disabilities Act; Animal Rights Law; The Law of Attachment and Garnishment; Bankruptcy Law for the Individual Debtor; Individual Bankruptcy and Restructuring; Banks and their Customers; Buying and Selling Your Home; The Law of Buying and Selling; The Law of Capital Punishment; The Law of Child Custody; Your Rights in a Class Action Suit; Commercial Law; Consumer Rights Law; The Law of Contracts; Copyright Law; Credit Cards and the Law; The Law of Debt Collection; Dictionary of Selected Legal Terms; The Law of Dispute Resolution; Drunk Driving Law; DWI, DUI and the Law; Education Law; Elder Law; Employee Rights in the Workplace; Employment Discrimination Under Title VII; Environmental Law; Estate Planning; Everyday Legal Forms; Executors and Personal Representatives: Rights and Responsibilities; Harassment in the Workplace; Health Care and Your Rights. Home Mortgage Law Primer; Hos-

ABOUT THE AUTHOR

pital Liability Law; Identity Theft and How To Protect Yourself; Insurance Law; The Law of Immigration; International Adoption; Juvenile Justice and Children's Law; Labor Law; Landlord-Tenant Law; The Law of Libel and Slander; Living Together: Practical Legal Issues; Marriage and Divorce; The Law of Medical Malpractice; Motor Vehicle Law; The Law of No-Fault Insurance; Nursing Home Negligence; The Law of Obscenity and Pornography; Patent Law; The Law of Personal Injury; The Law of Premises Liability; Prescription Drugs; Privacy and the Internet: Your Rights and Expectations Under the Law; Probate Law; The Law of Product Liability; Real Estate Law for the Homeowner and Broker; Religion and the Law; Retirement Planning; The Right to Die; Rights of Single Parents; Law for the Small Business Owner; Small Claims Court; Social Security Law; Special Education Law; The Law of Speech and the First Amendment; Teenagers and Substance Abuse; Trademark Law; Victim's Rights Law; The Law of Violence Against Women; Welfare: Your Rights and the Law; What if it Happened to You: Violent Crimes and Victims' Rights; What if the Product Doesn't Work: Warranties & Guarantees; Workers' Compensation Law; and Your Child's Legal Rights: An Overview.

INTRODUCTION

Most parents-to-be expect that their baby will be born into this world in good health, and continue through childhood physically and mentally fit. Unfortunately, that is not always the case. There are at least 12 million children in the United States who have special health care needs, most of whom live at home with their families. Many of these children have complex medical conditions and disabilities.

When you have a child with special needs, it can be overwhelming. How do you plan for your child's future? Where do you go for help? Will your child be able to go to school or get a job? What about health care and insurance? This almanac attempts to answer these questions.

This almanac discusses the legislation that has been enacted to protect disabled children and afford them certain rights under the law. The special education system is explored, and the expanded rights of disabled children to a free, appropriate education are discussed. The various services available to a challenged child are also explored, including early intervention programs.

This almanac also discusses the various estate planning techniques to assist parents of special needs children in preparing for their child's future.

The Appendix provides sample forms, and other pertinent information and data. The Glossary contains definitions of many of the terms used throughout the almanac.

CHAPTER 1:
CHILD ADVOCACY

REACH OUT

Every parent looks forward to the birth of a healthy child, therefore they are often devastated to learn that their child is disabled in some way. Feelings of anger and depression may follow. Parents often feel guilty because of their mixed emotions regarding their less than perfect child, or because they feel responsible in some way for the child's condition. Parents may also be in denial about the child's diagnosis. All of these feelings are normal while you learn to accept your child's condition, and make the emotional adjustment.

It is difficult parenting a child with special needs. Caring for a child with special needs leaves little time to eat and sleep, much less attend to other matters. This is especially hard when there are other children in the family who need your time and attention. Your schedule is likely crammed with visits to medical providers, speech therapists, physical therapists, occupational therapists, and school officials, to name a few. It is likely that you have asked yourself time and again how you have been able to cope, but somehow you do, because you can't give up on your special child.

Parent advocates advise those who find themselves caring for a child with special needs to connect with other parents who have had the same experiences. There are many organizations that bring together parents of challenged children, where you can compare notes and find that you are not alone.

If you have access to the internet, there are many websites, chat rooms and e-mail listservs where you can post your questions and concerns, and obtain valuable feedback and support from other parents. You will find that there are other parents who never get any sleep, who juggle work and medical appointments, and who have similar concerns about their future and the future of their child.

You can obtain valuable information on how to advocate for your child by hearing from parents who have experienced what you are experiencing. Soon you will find yourself working with other parents, and helping to improve care for all special needs children.

A directory of parent advocacy groups is set forth at Appendix 1 and a directory of national disability organizations is set forth at Appendix 2.

WHAT IS AN ADVOCATE?

An advocate is generally defined as one who defends and argues on behalf of people or causes. Advocates pinpoint and describe problems, and then find solutions to those problems. Although a disabled child's parents are often the child's strongest advocates, there are a number of different types of advocates who may be able to assist you in protecting your child.

For example, special education teachers are advocates for their students, and work hard to improve the lives of children with disabilities and their families. Educational advocates evaluate children with disabilities and make recommendations about services, supports and special education programs.

Lay advocates use specialized knowledge and expertise to help parents resolve problems with schools. They are usually knowledgeable about legal rights and responsibilities, and often represent parents in special education hearings. Advocates know the procedures that parents must follow to protect their rights and the child's rights under the law.

YOU ARE YOUR CHILD'S MOST EFFECTIVE ADVOCATE

Parents are the most effective advocates for their children. Parents know their children better than anyone else. From birth, parents serve as role models and teachers for their child, and have their best interests at heart. This is a life-long commitment.

Studies show that parents who advocate for their child are best able to cope with their child's special needs. Advocating means standing up to your child's teachers, medical providers, and therapists to make sure your child gets good care. In order to be able to advocate effectively, you must gain as much knowledge as possible about your child's condition. Meet with school officials on a regular basis to discuss your child's progress and goals. You must be involved to make sure all of your child's needs are met.

In addition to the information you gather from your child's medical providers, do your own research. There is a wealth of information available on the internet. Make sure you understand all aspects of your child's condition so you can understand and evaluate what you are told by medical providers and school authorities.

Unfortunately, doctors are often too busy to sit down and thoroughly explain all aspects of your child's diagnosis and treatment, and to answer the multitude of questions that are sure to arise. Therefore, you must become your own expert to the best of your ability. You are your child's most ardent advocate.

You must also become knowledgeable about your child's health insurance benefits, and the availability of services for your child. Special needs children are entitled to a wide range of services under state laws. Find out for yourself what your child is entitled to under the law instead of relying on others, who may be misinformed or unaware of the available services. Become familiar with your rights and responsibilities under the primary disability laws, which are discussed more fully in this almanac.

In order to be an effective advocate, you should prepare a plan for your child's future. What are the short-term and long-term goals you foresee for your child, and how do you plan on helping your child achieve those goals? Do you expect your child to achieve independence, get a job, marry, have children? You must be both optimistic and realistic. Your plan must detail the services and supports your child will need to meet the goals you envision for his or her future.

PROTECTING YOUR CHILD FROM ABUSE

Sadly, there are individuals who prey upon those who cannot protect themselves. Therefore, you must be vigilant in protecting your child from such predators, particularly younger children and children who have more severe disabilities and an inability to communicate effectively.

Research shows that disabled children are more likely to be abused than healthy children. This is in large part due to the fact that many disabled children are dependent on caregivers to help them with daily activities, such as bathing, dressing, and eating. A disabled child may not understand that they are a victim of abuse, and may be unable to communicate well enough to alert their parents or other authorities.

The potential for abuse is even greater for a child who is living away from home where the parent is not able to monitor the child's behavior. In fact, many abusers look for work that brings them in close contact with children, particularly the most vulnerable children. Such a child may misinterpret predatory behavior, particularly if they have developed an emotional tie to the abuser, and not even realize they are victims of abuse. Some children may be afraid to speak up, especially if they have been threatened and don't know where to turn for help.

For these reasons, you must be aware of certain warning signs that may indicate your child is a victim of abuse. For example, if your child seems especially fearful around a particular caregiver, this may indicate a problem. You should also watch for sudden changes in your child's personality, such as anxiety, depression, and aggressiveness. Your child may appear withdrawn and unable to sleep or eat. You must also check your child for unexplained bruises or injuries, particularly to private body parts. You must try to teach your child to recognize and report abuse.

If your child is living in a residential facility, find out what their policies and procedures are regarding child protection. What is their hiring policy? How thoroughly do they investigate prospective employees? Also, find out whether you will be contacted if a problem arises, particularly if your child is the victim of abuse. If you suspect your child is the victim of abuse, you must immediately contact your local law enforcement authorities and child protection agency.

PREPARING YOUR CHILD FOR EMERGENCIES AND DISASTERS

Recent tragic events have alerted society to the importance of having a plan in place in case an emergency or disaster were to occur. Planning ahead is even more important when you are the parent of a special needs child. If your child has special health care needs, your plan will likely be more complex. Many children with serious medical conditions and special requirements are discharged from the hospital much earlier than in the past, along with their medication and medical equipment.

Many disabled children cannot be moved easily or quickly due to their condition, and are oftentimes attached to necessary medical equipment. The equipment itself may depend on electricity to work, such as a ventilator to assist the child in breathing, or a feeding tube to provide the child with necessary nutrients. Many children rely on walkers or wheelchairs to move around. Also, it is not unusual for a special needs child to become anxious or upset when their routine is broken.

The American Academy of Pediatrics (AAP) and the American College of Emergency Physicians have recognized the importance of making an emergency plan to protect this most vulnerable population. Following are some suggestions to consider in devising your plan.

At Home

Emergency Instructions

It is important that every person in your household, including in-home caregivers, is instructed on what to do in case of an emergency. A one-page emergency instruction sheet should be prepared and should include information about exits, fire extinguishers, power shut-offs, emergency phone numbers, etc. The emergency instruction sheet should be posted in a place where it can be seen.

Supplies

You should keep a box containing flashlights, water, blankets, and other necessities close to an exit. Your child's medicine, medical records and medical equipment must also be stored in an area that is easily accessible in case you have to suddenly leave your home.

Contacts

Advise your local electric company that you have a special needs child who depends on electricity so that your home will be a priority when restoring electricity. In case of an electrical failure, you should have a back-up generator to power your child's medical equipment during the outage.

You should also contact your local emergency center, such as the fire department, to find out what services are available for your child in case of an emergency. For example, ask if they would be able to supply you with a back-up generator in case of a power failure?

For children with more serious conditions, the best course of action may be to take them to the nearest hospital in case of a disaster. You should discuss this with your child's physician.

At School

Every special needs child should have a school emergency plan in place. The student's Individualized Education Program (IEP) should include the emergency plan and should be distributed to all school personnel. The person responsible for working with your child in school, such as their special education teacher or aide, should practice the plan with your child so he or she won't be overly anxious if an emergency occurs and their regular routine is interrupted. In addition, school bus staff should also have instructions on how to proceed in case of an emergency.

CHILD ADVOCACY

Away From Home

Your emergency plan should be left every place your child may frequent when he or she is not at home or in school, such as a child care center, camp, relative's home, etc. In addition, a copy of your emergency plan should be kept in your child's backpack.

CHAPTER 2: WHAT DOES IT MEAN TO BE A CHALLENGED CHILD?

IN GENERAL

A challenged child is generally defined as a child who has special health care needs. A challenged child is also referred to as a "special needs child," a term used interchangeably in this almanac. The child's needs may be physical, emotional, behavioral, or developmental. The child may suffer from a wide range of conditions, such as cerebral palsy, attention deficit disorder, autism, depression, cystic fibrosis, etc. The child may have been born with the condition, or may have developed a chronic illness or disability later in life.

The child's condition may range from mild to severe, and may encompass more than one problem. Once diagnosed, some children respond to routine treatment and monitoring, and are able to function quite normally. Others, with more significant problems, may need more extensive medical intervention for the rest of their lives.

It is estimated that over 12 million children in the United States have special health care needs. This represents approximately one in five households who are caring for a special needs child. Most special needs children reside at home with their family. Approximately four million students with disabilities are enrolled in public elementary and secondary schools in the United States. Of this total, 43 percent are students classified as learning disabled, 8 percent as emotionally disturbed, and 1 percent as other health impaired.

RATING MENTAL FUNCTIONING

Medical providers rely on a number of psychological tests to determine a child's mental functioning. In order to calculate a child's intelligence quotient (IQ), the child's mental age is divided by their chronological

WHAT DOES IT MEAN TO BE A CHALLENGED CHILD?

age, and multipled by one hundred. On the IQ scale, an IQ above 140 indicates genius level; an IQ between 100 and 120 indicates average to above average intelligence; and an IQ score under 90 generally indicates that the child has a mental deficiency.

Mental deficiency is further broken down into categories. For example, an IQ between 70 and 84 indicates a borderline deficiency; an IQ between 55 and 69 is considered mild and thus educable; an IQ between 40 and 54 is considered moderate but trainable; an IQ between 25 and 39 indicates a severe mental deficiency; and an IQ below 25 is considered highly severe.

There are many factors which are believed to cause a mental deficiency. Heredity is considered a big factor. In addition, there are environmental factors that contribute to reduced mental functioning, such as brain injury and malnutrition. The greater the deficiency, the more developmental problems the child is expected to endure.

If you suspect your child has a mental deficiency, it is crucial that you seek a proper diagnosis as soon as possible so the child can benefit from early intervention programs. Such programs assist in the child's physical, emotional and social development. Delay in obtaining help for your child may result in more severe problems as the child grows, and prevent the child from reaching his or her full potential.

AUTISM

Autisim is a developmental disability significantly affecting verbal and nonverbal communication and social interaction, generally evident before age 3, that adversely affects a child's educational performance. Other characteristics often associated with autism are engagement in repetitive activities and stereotyped movements, resistance to environmental change or change in daily routines, and unusual responses to sensory experiences.

ACQUIRED IMMUNE DEFICIENCY SYNDROME (AIDS)

Acquired Immune Deficiency Syndrome (AIDS) is caused by infection of the individual with a human immunodeficiency virus (HIV) that alters a person's immune system and damages his/her ability to fight off other diseases. AIDS is primarily spread by sexual contact and the sharing of contaminated needles and syringes among users of illegal intravenous drugs. Children generally acquire the disease in one of two other ways:

    1. The HIV virus can be passed on from infected mothers during pregnancy, at birth, or shortly after birth. This is the most common way that children contract AIDS.

2. In a small number of cases, the HIV virus has been spread through blood products and blood transfusions. However, since blood donation screening has increased significantly, the chance of getting AIDS in this manner is extremely small.

EMOTIONAL DISTURBANCE

Emotional disturbance is generally defined as a condition exhibiting one or more of the following characteristics over a long period of time and to a marked degree that adversely affects a child's educational performance:

1. An inability to learn that cannot be explained by intellectual, sensory, or health factors.

2. An inability to build or maintain satisfactory interpersonal relationships with peers and teachers.

3. Inappropriate types of behavior or feelings under normal circumstances.

4. A general pervasive mood of unhappiness or depression.

5. A tendency to develop physical symptoms or fears associated with personal or school problems.

The term includes schizophrenia. The term does not apply to children who are socially maladjusted, unless it is determined that they have an emotional disturbance.

LEARNING DISABILITIES

The Education for All Handicapped Children Act defines a learning disability (LD) as a "disorder in one or more of the basic psychological processes involved in understanding or using language, spoken or written, which may manifest itself in an imperfect ability to listen, think, speak, read, write, spell or do mathematical calculations."

The definition further states that LD includes perceptual handicaps, brain injury, minimal brain dysfunction, dyslexia, and developmental aphasia. According to the law, LD does not include learning problems that are primarily the result of visual, hearing, or motor handicaps; mental retardation; or environmental, cultural, or economic disadvantage. Also required is a severe discrepancy between the child's potential—as measured by IQ—and his or her current skill level—as measured by achievement tests.

It is estimated that anywhere from 1% to 30% of the general population exhibit learning disabilities, a result which appears to reflect the variations in definitions of the term "learning disabled." However, the most widely agreed upon estimate is 2% to 3%.

Children who are learning disabled may exhibit a wide range of traits, including poor reading comprehension, spoken language, writing, and reasoning ability. Hyperactivity, inattention, and perceptual coordination problems may also be associated with LD, but are not examples of LD. Other traits that may be present include a variety of symptoms of brain dysfunction, including uneven and unpredictable test performance, perceptual impairments, motor disorders, and emotional characteristics such as impulsiveness, low tolerance for frustration, and maladjustment.

MENTAL RETARDATION

Mental retardation is basically defined as significantly subaverage general intellectual functioning, existing concurrently with deficits in adaptive behavior and manifested during the developmental period, that adversely affects a child's educational performance.

MULTIPLE DISABILITIES

Multiple disabilities refers to concomitant impairments—e.g., mental retardation-blindness, mental retardation-orthopedic impairment, etc.—the combination of which causes such severe educational needs that they cannot be accommodated in special education programs solely for one of the impairments. However, the term does not include deaf-blindness.

ORTHOPEDIC IMPAIRMENTS

A severe orthopedic impairment that adversely affects a child's educational performance may include those impairments caused by congenital anomalies, such as clubfoot; impairments caused by disease, such as poliomyelitis; and impairments from other causes, such as cerebral palsy, amputations, and fractures or burns that cause contractures.

TRAUMATIC BRAIN INJURY

Traumatic brain injury generally refers to an acquired injury to the brain caused by an external physical force, resulting in total or partial functional disability or psychosocial impairment, or both. The term applies to open or closed head injuries resulting in impairments in one or more areas, such as cognition; language; memory; attention; reasoning; abstract thinking; judgment; problem-solving; sensory, perceptual, and motor abilities; psychosocial behavior; physical functions; information processing; and speech. The term does not apply to brain injuries that are congenital or degenerative, or to brain injuries induced by birth trauma.

HEARING IMPAIRMENT

An impairment in hearing, depending on its severity, whether permanent or fluctuating, may adversely affect a child's educational performance because the child is impaired in processing linguistic information through hearing.

VISUAL IMPAIRMENT

A visual impairment, even with correction, is one which adversely affects a child's performance. The degree of blindness ranges from total loss to a fair degree of vision. Therefore all visually impaired children cannot be treated alike. Their individual problems and needs must be taken into consideration.

DEAF-BLINDNESS

A child who suffers serious combined hearing and visual impairments have communication and other developmental and educational problems such that the child cannot be accommodated in special education programs solely for children with deafness or children with blindness.

SPEECH OR LANGUAGE IMPAIRMENTS

Speech or language impairments which affect communication include stuttering, impaired articulation, a language impairment, or a voice impairment.

OTHER HEALTH IMPAIRMENTS

Children may also suffer from other chronic or acute health problems that limit their strength, vitality or alertness, including asthma, diabetes, epilepsy, a heart condition, hemophilia, lead poisoning, leukemia, nephritis, rheumatic fever, and sickle cell anemia.

ATTENTION DEFICIT HYPERACTIVITY DISORDER (ADHD)

One of the most commonly diagnosed conditions in school age children today is attention deficit hyperactivity disorder (ADHD)—a term which is used interchangeably with attention deficit disorder (ADD). ADHD is a complex disorder which is defined in the fourth edition of the Diagnostic and Statistical Manual (DSM-IV) of the American Psychiatric Association as "a disorder that can include a

WHAT DOES IT MEAN TO BE A CHALLENGED CHILD?

list of nine specific symptoms of inattention and nine symptoms of hyperactivity/impulsivity."

The specific DSM-IV criteria for Attention Deficit Hyperactivity Disorder are set forth at Appendix 3.

A child must exhibit several characteristics to be clinically diagnosed as having ADHD:

1. Severity—The behavior in question must occur more frequently in the child than in other children at the same developmental stage;

2. Early Onset—At least some of the symptoms must have been present prior to age 7;

3. Duration—The symptoms must also have been present for at least 6 months prior to the evaluation;

4. Impact—The symptoms must have a negative impact on the child's academic or social life; and

Statistics

Statistics demonstrate that about 1% to 3% of the school-aged population has the full ADHD syndrome, without symptoms of other disorders; another 5% to 10% of the school-aged population have a partial ADHD syndrome or one with other problems, such as anxiety and depression present; and another 15% to 20% of the school-aged population may show transient, subclinical, or masquerading behaviors suggestive of ADHD. Boys are about three times more likely than girls to have symptoms of ADHD.

Statistics also demonstrate that approximately 50% of children with ADHD can be taught in the regular classroom. Teachers must be trained to recognize the special needs of these students and to make any appropriate teaching and classroom modifications. The other 50% will require some degree of special education and related services.

Of the latter 50%, about 35-40% will primarily be served in the regular classroom with additional support, or receive some special services outside of the classroom. The most severely affected, 10-15%, may require self-contained classrooms.

Causation

Commonly suspected causes of ADHD have included toxins, developmental impairments, diet, injury, ineffective parenting and heredity. While there is no biological or psychological test that makes a definitive diagnosis of ADHD, a diagnosis can be made based on a clinical history of abnormality and impairment.

Treatment

There are two modalities of treatment presently in use for ADHD. Psychostimulants—such as ritalin—are the most widely used medications for the management of ADHD symptoms. Behavior modification techniques have also been used to treat the behavioral symptoms of ADHD. A thorough medical examination is also important to rule out other possible causes of ADHD like symptoms.

Educational Intervention

Laws passed during the last five years have mandated educational interventions for children with ADHD. Today, modifications and special placements in public school settings are part of treatment of ADHD. It has been recognized that children with ADHD are at risk for school failure and emotional difficulties. However, early identification and intervention has demonstrated that these children can overcome many of these hurdles and achieve success.

HIDDEN DISABILITIES

Parents should be aware of hidden disabilities. Hidden disabilities are physical or mental impairments that are not readily apparent. A disability such as a limp, paralysis, total blindness or deafness is usually obvious to others, but hidden disabilities such as low vision, poor hearing, heart disease, or chronic illness may not be so obvious. These hidden disabilities often cannot be readily known without the administration of appropriate diagnostic tests.

CHAPTER 3:
EARLY INTERVENTION SERVICES

WHAT IS EARLY INTERVENTION?

Early intervention services are special services for eligible infants and toddlers under the age of 3, who have developmental delays or disabilities. Early intervention programs are designed to identify and meet children's needs in five developmental areas including:

1. Physical development;
2. Cognitive development;
3. Communication;
4. Social or emotional development; and
5. Adaptive development.

Under the Individuals with Disabilities Education Act (IDEA), the states are required to provide services to infants and toddlers who have special needs. However, each state develops its own policies for carrying out the program.

ELIGIBILITY

Under the IDEA, a child who is diagnosed with a physical or mental condition, and who is either experiencing a developmental delay or is at risk of having a developmental delay, would be eligible for early intervention services.

Developmental delay means that the child is developing slower than normal in one or more areas. For example, the child may not be talking or walking at an age when most children are doing so. At risk means the child's development may be delayed unless early intervention services are provided. Some children do not develop at the same pace as other children, however, this does not automatically mean the child is in need of services.

EARLY INTERVENTION SERVICES

A child development checklist is set forth at Appendix 4.

Under the IDEA, a complete evaluation of the child is necessary to decide whether he or she has a disability or a developmental delay, or is at risk of having a disability or delay. In order to obtain an evaluation, you must contact the agency that is in charge of the state's early intervention program.

A directory of state special education agencies is set forth at Appendix 5.

THE EVALUATION PROCESS

Once you have contacted the appropriate agency, you will be assigned to a temporary service coordinator who will guide you and your child through the evaluation process. The evaluation is provided at no cost. The coordinator generally has a background in early childhood development, and has information on all of the services in your state.

The evaluation consists of a multidisciplinary assessment of your child carried out by qualified professionals who have different areas of training and experience, e.g., speech, hearing, vision, physical abilities, etc. The purpose of the evaluation is to find out whether or not your child is eligible for early intervention services.

As part of the evaluation, the multidisciplinary team will gather information about your child, e.g., by observing your child, and asking your child to perform age-appropriate tasks. Following the evaluation, you will meet with the team and go over the results. If it is determined that your child does have a diagnosed physical or mental condition, a developmental delay, or is at risk, he or she would be eligible for early intervention services.

ASSESSMENT

If your child is eligible for services, he or she will then be assessed, in order to identify your child's unique strengths and needs, and determine what services will be provided to meet those needs. As part of the assessment process, certain records and reports concerning your child will be considered, including but not limited to:

1. Doctor's reports;

2. Results from developmental tests and performance assessments given to your child;

3. Your child's medical and developmental history;

4. Direct observations and feedback from all members of the multidisciplinary team, including the parents; and

5. Interviews with the family and caretakers.

A family assessment will also take place to identify whether there are any supports and services that will enhance the family's ability to meet the child's developmental needs. This assessment is usually conducted in the manner of an interview with the child's family.

THE INDIVIDUALIZED FAMILY SERVICE PLAN (IFSP)

After the assessment is concluded, a written plan will be developed which sets forth the early intervention services that will be provided to your child, and to the family, if needed. The plan is called an Individualized Family Service Plan (IFSP).

Your child's IFSP must include the following:

1. Your child's present physical, cognitive, communication, social/emotional, and adaptive development levels and needs;

2. Family information including the family's resources, priorities, and concerns;

3. The major outcomes expected to be achieved under the plan;

4. The specific services your child will be receiving;

5. The location where the services will be provided, e.g. home, hospital, etc. To the extent possible, services are to be provided in the child's natural environment—i.e., where the child lives, learns, and plays.

6. The number of days or sessions your child will receive, and the length of each session.

7. Whether the service will be provided on a one-on-one or group basis;

8. The party responsible for paying for the services;

9. The name of the service coordinator overseeing the implementation of the IFSP; and

10. The steps to be taken to support your child's transition out of early intervention and into another program when the time comes.

Depending on your child's needs, his or her early intervention services may include:

1. Family training, counseling, and home visits;

2. Special instruction;

3. Speech therapy;

EARLY INTERVENTION SERVICES

4. Hearing impairment services;

5. Occupational therapy;

6. Physical therapy;

7. Psychological services;

8. Medical services for diagnostic or evaluation purposes;

9. Health services needed to enable your child to benefit from the other services;

10. Social work services;

11. Assistive technology devices and services;

12. Transportation;

13. Nutrition services; and

14. Service coordination services.

COSTS

The cost of any specific services under the plan depends on your state's policies, however, under the IDEA, the following services must be provided at no cost:

1. Child Find services;

2. Evaluations and assessments;

3. The development and review of the Individualized Family Service Plan; and

4. Service coordination.

Depending on your state's policies, you may have to pay for certain other services. Some services may be covered by your health insurance, or by Medicaid. Nevertheless, services cannot be denied to a child just because his or her family is not able to pay for them.

AGING OUT OF THE EARLY INTERVENTION PROGRAM

When your child turns 3, he or she is no longer eligible for the early intervention program. Your family's service coordinator will assist you in making the transition to your state's special education program designed to provide services to eligible pre-schoolers, if there is still a need for such services at that time. A transition plan meeting must take place at least 90 days before a child turns three. The transition plan will identify the services the child may need.

EARLY INTERVENTION SERVICES

The service coordinator will ask the family to sign a permission form so the next agency or service provider can be contacted to plan for transition. A meeting among the family, the service coordinator, and the local school district will be arranged. The school district will determine whether the child is eligible for preschool special education services. Following evaluation and testing, if a child is eligible, their services will be provided through an Individual Education Program (IEP).

EARLY HEARING DETECTION AND INTERVENTION PROGRAM

Each state has an Early Hearing Detection and Intervention Program (EHDI) to identify infants with a hearing impairment so they can receive intervention services as early as possible in the child's development. According to the Centers for Disease Control (CDC), if hearing loss is not identified until 2 or 3 years of age, your child may suffer delays in speech, language, and cognitive development.

EHDI programs are characterized by three main components:

1. Screening the infants for hearing loss;

2. Audiologic evaluation to confirm hearing loss;

3. Early intervention to enhance communication, thinking, and behavioral skills needed to achieve academic and social success.

The CDC guidelines state that all infants should be screened for hearing loss before 1 month of age, preferably before leaving the hospital following birth. Infants with risk indicators for progressive or delayed-onset hearing loss should receive audiologic monitoring every 6 months until age 3 years.

If your child does not pass the hearing screening, he or she will be referred for further testing to rule out or confirm a hearing loss. All infants with confirmed hearing loss will be referred for a comprehensive medical evaluation to assess the causes and look for potential or related disabilities. Depending on the results of the audiological and medical examinations, infants may be referred to an intervention program.

Diagnostic Testing

If an infant does not pass their hearing screening test following birth, they will be referred for additional testing by an audiologist. Diagnostic tests may include the following:

Auditory Brainstem Response (ABR) Test

An Auditory Brainstem Response (ABR) test checks the brain's response to sound and is measured by placing non-invasive electrodes on the head to record the brain's response to sound.

Otoacoustic Emissions (OAE) Test

An Otoacoustic Emissions test checks the inner ear response to sound and is measured by placing a very sensitive microphone in the ear canal to measure the ear's response to sound.

False Positives

Your child may receive a false positive following their hearing screening test. A false positive occurs when your infant does not have a hearing loss but does not pass the hearing screening. Hearing screening tests are not meant to diagnose hearing loss in infants. Instead, they are meant to find all infants that might have a hearing loss. Because they are not a diagnostic test, hearing screening tests sometimes misidentify infants as having a hearing loss.

In the United States, between 10 and 100 babies per 1,000 do not pass the screening test. Only one to three babies per 1,000 actually have hearing loss. This means that most of the babies referred for diagnostic testing will be shown to have no hearing loss.

CHAPTER 4:
YOUR CHILD'S RIGHT TO A FREE APPROPRIATE PUBLIC EDUCATION

EDUCATION LAW

Education law is derived from both federal and state sources. The United States Constitution is the governing law of the land, and many aspects of our current education law have evolved from its tenets. In addition, Congress has enacted a number of laws which deal with education. These laws are published in the United States Code by Title number. Education Law is published under Title 20 of the U.S. Code.

States must develop education statutes that are consistent with the United States Code (U.S.C.). State statutes may provide more rights than the corresponding federal law, but states may not give lesser rights than those provided for by federal law.

Regulations are enacted to clarify and explain statutes. Although regulations may give force and effect to a statute, they must also be consistent with the statute. Federal Regulations are published in the Code of Federal Regulations (CFR).

For example, Title 20 of the U. S. Code requires the U. S. Department of Education to develop and publish special education regulations giving force and effect to the Individuals with Disabilities Education Act (the "IDEA"). States must also develop special education regulations that are consistent with the Code of Federal Regulations.

COMPULSORY EDUCATION

Historically, poor children did not attend school regularly, and often dropped out before graduation. In an effort to make sure all children attended school, state legislatures passed compulsory attendance laws. Under these laws, parents were obligated to send their children to school or face prosecution. Presently, all children who fall between a state's age range for compulsory education are required to attend school on a regular basis. Children generally begin their formal education at age 6. In most states, the maximum age a child is required to attend school is 16.

A table setting forth the compulsory education age range, by state, is set forth at Appendix 6.

COMPULSORY SPECIAL EDUCATION

Disabled children, however, were often either absent from school or not enrolled at all. Disabled children who did attend school were generally put into special education classes with other disabled children, regardless of the nature or extent of their disabilities. Disabled children were never placed in classes with non-disabled children.

Despite the compulsory attendance laws, most states allowed school authorities to exclude children if they believed that the child would not benefit from education, or if the child's presence would disrupt the non-disabled children or interfere with teaching. In fact, in some states, it was actually illegal for a parent to enroll a disabled child in public school once that child had been excluded.

In an effort to make sure all disabled children are afforded an education, state legislatures passed compulsory special education laws under which schools are obligated to provide special education services to all children. Presently, all children who fall between a state's age range for compulsory special education services are entitled to receive a free, appropriate education. Generally, the ages for compulsory special education services begins early, e.g., from birth to 3 years old in some states, and ends later, e.g. 21 years old in most states.

A table setting forth the compulsory special education services age range, by state, is set forth at Appendix 7.

VOCATIONAL SCHOOLS

The predecessor to present-day special education programs was the "vocational" school. Vocational schools were more likely to be found in the urban environment. The students were generally children from depressed areas who were perceived as unable to function in a purely academic program. Often, such children were labeled as "learning disabled."

These children were generally not steered towards college and, in many cases, actually discouraged from pursuing higher education, because college was not seen as a likely prospect for their future. The vocational training was designed to prevent delinquency and give these underprivileged children the necessary training to enable them to enter the skilled labor workforce upon graduation from high school.

STATE EDUCATIONAL SYSTEMS

When advocating for a disabled child, it is helpful to understand the educational system under which your child's school operates, including how it works and the parties responsible for making sure it works. At the state level, a local school district—also known as a local education agency ("LEA")—is generally governed by a state governmental entity known as a Board of Education ("Board").

The Board is generally made up of members who are elected by the citizens of the particular district. The Board is responsible for overseeing the educational process within its jurisdiction, including formulating education budgets, establishing policies and procedures, hiring certain officials, such as the superintendent of schools, and making sure that there is compliance with state and federal education laws.

Most states have intermediate school districts made up of districts which are in geographic proximity to one another. Intermediate school districts share their respective resources in order to provide certain services which individually they would not be able to undertake, such as special education programs, technical education programs, and health services.

The intermediate school district is also responsible for evaluating, at public expense, all students suspected of having disabilities from birth through twenty-one years of age, regardless of whether they attend public or private school. This function is known as "child find" which is discussed more fully below.

THE SPECIAL EDUCATION PROCESS

More than five million children receive special education services. Approximately 2.5 million of these children have learning disabilities. Others suffer speech and language disabilities; autism; attention deficit disorder (ADD), hearing and visual impairments, emotional disturbance and mental retardation.

Child Find

In order to identify, locate, and evaluate all children with disabilities in the state who need special education and related services, the state must conduct "Child Find" activities. A child may be identified by "Child Find," and parents may be asked if the "Child Find" system can evaluate their child. Parents can also call the "Child Find" system and ask that their child be evaluated. In other cases, the school professional may ask that a child be evaluated to see if he or she has a disability. Parents may also contact the child's teacher or other school professional to ask that their child be evaluated. This request may be verbal or in writing.

Parental consent is needed before the child may be evaluated, and the evaluation needs to be completed within a reasonable time after the parent gives consent. The evaluation must assess the child in all areas related to the child's suspected disability. The evaluation results are used to decide the child's eligibility for special education and related services and to make decisions about an appropriate educational program for the child. If the parents disagree with the evaluation, they have the right to take their child for an Independent Educational Evaluation (IEE), and can ask that the school system pay for this IEE.

A group of qualified professionals, along with the parents, look at the child's evaluation results. They decide if the child is a "child with a disability," as defined by The Individuals with Disabilities Education Act (IDEA). Parents may ask for a hearing to challenge the eligibility decision. If the child is found to be a "child with a disability," as defined by IDEA, he or she is eligible for special education and related services.

The IEP Meeting

Within 30 calendar days after a child is determined eligible for special education and related services, the team of professionals must meet to write an Individualized Education Program (IEP) for the child. The school system must schedule and conduct the IEP meeting. School staff must:

1. Contact the participants, including the parents;

2. Notify parents early enough to make sure they have an opportunity to attend;

3. Schedule the meeting at a time and place agreeable to parents and the school;

4. Tell the parents the purpose, time, and location of the meeting;

5. Tell the parents who will be attending; and

6. Tell the parents that they may invite people to the meeting who have knowledge or special expertise about the child.

At the meeting, the IEP team discusses the child's needs and writes the IEP. Parents—and the student, if appropriate—are part of the team.

Consent

Before the school system may provide special education and related services to the child for the first time, the parents must give consent.

The child begins to receive services as soon as possible after the meeting. If the parents do not agree with the IEP and placement, they may discuss their concerns with other members of the IEP team and try to work out an agreement. If they still disagree, parents can ask for mediation, or the school may offer mediation. Parents may also file a complaint with the state education agency and may request a due process hearing, at which time mediation must be available.

Services

The school is obligated to make sure that the child's IEP is being carried out as it was written. Parents are given a copy of the IEP. Each of the child's teachers and service providers has access to the IEP and knows his or her specific responsibilities for carrying out the IEP. This includes the accommodations, modifications, and supports that must be provided to the child, in keeping with the IEP.

Progress Reports

The child's progress toward the annual goals is measured, as stated in the IEP. His or her parents are regularly informed of their child's progress and whether that progress is enough for the child to achieve the goals by the end of the year. These progress reports must be given to parents at least as often as parents are informed of a nondisabled children's progress.

Annual Review

The child's IEP is reviewed by the IEP team at least once a year, or more often if the parents or school ask for a review. If necessary, the IEP is revised. Parents, as team members, must be invited to attend these meetings. Parents can make suggestions for changes, can agree or disagree with the IEP goals, and agree or disagree with the placement.

If parents do not agree with the IEP and placement, they may discuss their concerns with other members of the IEP team and try to work out an agreement. As with the initial placement, if they still disagree, parents can ask for mediation, or file a complaint with the state education agency and request a due process hearing.

Reevaluation

At least every three years the child must be reevaluated. This evaluation is often called a "triennial." Its purpose is to find out if the child continues to be a "child with a disability," as defined by IDEA, and what the child's educational needs are. However, the child must be reevaluated more often if conditions warrant or if the child's parent or teacher asks for a new evaluation.

Stay Put Provision

Under the law, a child is required to remain in his or her current IEP placement pending any proposed changes or opposition to the placement. This is known as the "stay put" provision. Because the review process can be lengthy and time-consuming, parents who disagree with their child's placement sometimes unilaterally, at their own expense, place their child in another program without first obtaining consent. The parents then seek reimbursement of the expenses from the school district. However, if the courts determine that the child's IEP was appropriate, reimbursement will be denied.

THE INDIVIDUALIZED EDUCATION PROGRAM (IEP)

The Individualized Education Program (IEP) is a very important document for children with disabilities, and for those who are involved in educating them. Each child's IEP describes, among other things, the educational program that has been designed to meet that child's unique needs. Each child's IEP is different and is prepared for that child alone. The IEP must include certain information about the child and the individualized education program designed to meet his or her unique needs, as follows:

Current Performance

The IEP must state how the child is currently doing in school, known as present levels of educational performance. This information usually comes from results of classroom tests and assignments, individual tests given to decide eligibility for services or during reevaluation, and observations made by parents, teachers, related service providers, and other school staff. The statement about "current performance" includes how the child's disability affects his or her involvement and progress in the general curriculum.

Annual Goals

Annual goals refers to those goals that the child can reasonably accomplish in a year. The goals are broken down into short-term objectives or benchmarks. Goals may be academic, address social or behavioral needs, relate to physical needs, or address other educational needs. The goals must be measurable, i.e., it must be possible to measure whether the student has achieved the goals.

Special Education and Related Services

The IEP must list the special education and related services to be provided to the child or on behalf of the child. This includes supplementary aids and services that the child needs. It also includes modifications to the program or supports for school personnel—such as training or professional development—that will be provided to assist the child.

Participation with Nondisabled Children

The IEP must explain the extent, if any, to which the child will not participate with nondisabled children in the regular class and other school activities.

Participation in State and District Tests

Most states and districts give achievement tests to children in certain grades or age groups. The IEP must state what modifications in the administration of these tests the child will need. If a test is not appropriate for the child, the IEP must state why the test is not appropriate and how the child will be tested instead.

Dates and Places of Services

The IEP must state when services will begin, how often they will be provided, where they will be provided, and how long they will last.

Need for Transition Services

Beginning when the child is age 14, the IEP must address the courses he or she needs to take to reach his or her post-school goals. A statement of the need for transition services must also be included in each of the child's subsequent IEPs. Beginning when the child is age 16 (or younger, the IEP must state what transition services are needed to help the child prepare for leaving school.

Beginning at least one year before the child reaches the age of majority, the IEP must include a statement that the student has been told of any rights that will transfer to him or her at the age of majority. However, this statement would be needed only in states that transfer rights at the age of majority.

Progress

The IEP must state how the child's progress will be measured and how parents will be informed of that progress.

A sample Individualized Education Program is set forth at Appendix 8.

THE IEP TEAM MEMBERS

The law requires that certain individuals be involved in writing a child's IEP. An IEP team member may fill more than one of the team positions. if properly qualified and designated. For example, the school system representative may also be the person who can interpret the child's evaluation results. IEP team members include:

Parents

Parents are key members of the IEP team because they know their child very well and can talk about their child's strengths and needs, as well as their ideas for enhancing their child's education. If the parents are deaf or have limited proficiency in the English language, the school district must make reasonable efforts to arrange for an interpreter to be present at the IEP meeting so that the parents are able to participate fully in the process.

Teachers

Teachers are vital participants in the IEP meeting as well. At least one of the child's regular education teachers must be on the IEP team if the child is participating in the regular education environment. The child's special education teacher is also a member of the team, and contributes important information and experience about how to educate children with disabilities.

The special education teacher also has the responsibility of working with the student to carry out the IEP. He or she may work with the student in a resource room or special class devoted to students receiving special education services; team teach with the regular education teacher; and/or work with other school staff, e.g., the regular education teacher, to provide expertise in addressing the child's unique needs.

Evaluation Results Interpreter

Another important member of the IEP team is the individual who can interpret what the child's evaluation results mean in terms of designing appropriate instruction. The evaluation results are very useful in determining how the child is currently doing in school and the child's areas of need.

School District Representative

The individual representing the school district is the team member who knows a great deal about special education services and educating children with disabilities, and can discuss the necessary school resources. It is important that this individual have the authority to commit resources and be able to ensure that whatever services are set out in the IEP will actually be provided.

Related Services Professionals

The IEP team may also include additional individuals with knowledge or special expertise about the child. The parents or the school system can invite these individuals to participate on the team. Parents, for example, may invite an advocate who knows the child, or a professional with special expertise about the child and his or her disability, who can talk about the child's strengths and/or needs. The school system may invite one or more individuals who can offer special expertise or knowledge about the child, such as a paraprofessional or related services professional.

Because an important part of developing an IEP is considering a child's need for related services, related service professionals are often involved as IEP team members or participants. They share their special expertise about the child's needs and how their own professional services can address those needs. Depending on the child's individual needs, some related service professionals attending the IEP meeting or otherwise helping to develop the IEP may include occupational or physical therapists, psychologists, or speech-language pathologists.

The Student

The student may also be a member of the IEP team. If transition services are going to be discussed at the meeting, the student must be invited to attend.

RELATED SERVICES

A child may require related services in order to benefit from special education. Related services, as listed under the IDEA, include, but are not limited to:

1. Audiology services;
2. Counseling services;
3. Early identification and assessment of disabilities in children;
4. Medical services;
5. Occupational therapy;
6. Orientation and mobility services;
7. Parent counseling and training;
8. Physical therapy;
9. Psychological services;
10. Recreation;
11. Rehabilitation counseling services;
12. School health services;
13. Social work services in schools;

14. Speech-language pathology services; and

15. Transportation.

If a child needs a particular related service in order to benefit from special education, the related service professional should be involved in developing the IEP. He or she may be invited by the school or parent to join the IEP team as a person "with knowledge or special expertise about the child."

RIGHT TO TRANSPORTATION

As set forth above, students who receive special education services are entitled, without cost, to needed transportation to and from school, and school-related activities, such as class field trips and sporting events. In addition, if there is a charge for transportation to an optional field trip or event, a special needs child cannot be charged any more than the other students.

The IEP Team, including the parents, is responsible for determining the child's transportation needs, and listing the specific type of transportation as a "related service" in the child's IEP. This may include school bus service, van, door-to-door service, an aide to watch over the child, etc. The particular type of transportation must be appropriate for the child, taking into account the child's age and disability. For example, if the child uses a wheelchair, a bus or van with a lift should be specified. Another factor which must be taken into consideration is the length of the bus ride, particularly if the child has behavior problems or health problems that would make a long ride difficult.

If your child attends private school, he or she generally has the same rights as a child who is receiving special services in the district, including free, appropriate transportation. In general, schools must provide free transportation to and from private schools and on field trips if the school district provides transportation to public school students of the same age; the private school is within 10 miles of the school district boundaries; and the school is non-profit. If a student is placed in a residential school, he or she is also entitled to free transportation on school holidays and vacation periods.

SPECIAL FACTORS

Depending on the needs of the child, the IEP team needs to consider what the law calls "special factors," as follows:

Behavior

If the child's behavior interferes with his or her learning or the learning of others, the IEP team will consider strategies and supports to address the child's behavior.

English Proficiency

If the child has limited proficiency in English, the IEP team will consider the child's language needs as these needs relate to his or her IEP.

Blindness or Visual Impairment

If the child is blind or visually impaired, the IEP team must provide for instruction in Braille or the use of Braille, unless it determines after an appropriate evaluation that the child does not need this instruction.

Communication Needs

If the child has communication needs, the IEP team must consider those needs. For example, if the child is deaf or hearing impaired, the IEP team will consider his or her language and communication needs. This includes the child's opportunities to communicate directly with classmates and school staff in his or her usual method of communication, e.g., sign language.

Assistive Technology

The IEP team must also consider the child's need for assistive technology devices or services. Assistive technology devices and services are discussed more fully below.

PLACEMENT DECISIONS

The decision regarding a child's placement is made by a group of people who know the child, can interpret the evaluation results, and are familiar with appropriate types of placement. In some states, the IEP team serves as the group making the placement decision. In other states, this decision may be made by another group of people. In all cases, the parents have the right to be members of the group that decides the educational placement of the child.

Depending on the needs of the child, his or her IEP may be carried out in the regular class with supplementary aids and services, as needed; in a special class, where every student in the class is receiving special education services for some or all of the day; in a special school; at home; in a hospital or institution; or in another appropriate setting.

Nevertheless, placement decisions must be made according to IDEA's least restrictive environment (LRE) requirements. These requirements state that, to the maximum extent appropriate, children with disabilities must be educated with children who do not have disabilities, also known as "mainstreaming." Removal of children with disabilities from the regular educational environment may occur only if the nature or severity of the child's disability is such that education in regular classes with the use of supplementary aids and services cannot be achieved satisfactorily.

ACCESS TO THE IEP

After the IEP has been written, parents must receive a copy at no cost. The IDEA also states that everyone who will be involved in implementing the IEP must have access to the document including: (1) regular education teacher(s); (2) special education teacher(s); (3) related service provider(s); and (4) any other service provider responsible for a part of the child's education.

Each of these individuals needs to know what his or her specific responsibilities are for carrying out the child's IEP. This includes the specific accommodations, modifications, and supports that the child must receive, according to the IEP.

A directory of information sources about special education and the IEP process is set forth at Appendix 9.

TRANSITION SERVICES

Transition refers to activities meant to prepare students with disabilities for adult life. This can include developing postsecondary education and career goals, getting work experience while still in school, setting up linkages with adult service providers such as the vocational rehabilitation agency—whatever is appropriate for the student, given his or her interests, preferences, skills, and needs. As set forth above, statements about the student's transition needs must be included in the IEP after the student reaches a certain age.

Transitioning a special needs child from the school setting to the workplace is discussed more fully in Chapter 9 of this almanac.

ASSISTIVE TECHNOLOGY

As set forth above, a child's IEP must set forth any assistive technology devices or services that the child requires as part of their special education and related services. Assistive technology refers to any kind of technology that can be used to help a disabled person become more independent. The IDEA sets forth the school district's responsibility to provide assistive technology to students with disabilities if it is determined by an IEP team that the child needs it to benefit from his or her educational program. In addition, a child is allowed to take an assistive technology device home if it is needed to enable him or her to benefit from his educational program as determined the IEP team.

In order to determine whether a child needs assistive technology, an assessment should be undertaken where different types of technology are introduced to the child. If it is determined that the child would benefit from the device, selection of the device, and training in its use, should begin for the child and any other individuals who are involved with the child's development, including family, service providers, and teachers.

SCHOOL DISCIPLINE FOR DISABLED CHILDREN

Prior to the 1975 amendments to the Education of the Handicapped Act (EHA)—predecessor to the IDEA, the special educational needs of children with disabilities were not being met. School officials often used disciplinary measures to exclude disabled children from education simply because they were different or more difficult to educate than nondisabled children. When the IDEA was reauthorized in 1997, Congress recognized that in certain instances school districts needed increased flexibility to deal with safety issues while maintaining needed due process protections for these children.

The protections set forth in the IDEA regarding discipline are designed to prevent speculative and subjective decision making by school officials that led to widespread abuses of the rights of children with disabilities to an appropriate education in the past, e.g., where children were excluded entirely from education because they were identified as having a behavior problem.

The discipline provisions of the IDEA allow responsible and appropriate changes in placement of children with disabilities when their parents do not object. If school officials believe that a child's placement is inappropriate they can work with the child's parent through the IEP and placement processes to come up with an appropriate placement for the child that will meet the needs of the child and result in his or her improved learning and the learning of others and ensure a safe environment.

If a child has behavior problems that interfere with his or her learning or the learning of others, or commits an infraction that is not considered serious, schools can address the misconduct through appropriate instructional and/or related services, including conflict management, behavior management strategies, and measures, such as time-outs and restrictions in privileges, so long as they are not inconsistent with the child's IEP. If the IEP team determines that such services are needed, they must be added to the IEP and must be provided to the child.

Disciplinary Removal from Regular Placement

The provisions of the IDEA concerning the amount of time a child with a disability can be removed from his or her regular placement for disciplinary reasons only apply if the removal constitutes a change of placement and the parents object to the proposed action by school officials and request a due process hearing. These discipline rules are exceptions to the generally applicable requirement that a child remains in his or her current placement during the pendency of due process, and subsequent judicial, proceedings.

Even if the parents do not agree, school officials can generally remove any child with a disability from his or her regular school placement for up to 10 school days at a time whenever discipline is appropriate and is administered consistent with the treatment of nondisabled children. However, school officials cannot use this authority to repeatedly remove a child from his or her current placement if that series of removals means the child is removed for more than 10 school days in a school year, and factors such as the length of each removal, the total amount of time that the child is removed, and the proximity of the removals to one another lead to the conclusion that there has been a change in placement.

Beginning on the eleventh cumulative day in a school year that a child with a disability is removed from his or her current placement, the school district must provide those services determined to be necessary to enable the child to appropriately progress in the general curriculum and appropriately advance toward achieving the goals set out in the child's IEP. School personnel would determine where those services would be provided. This means that for the remainder of the removal that includes the eleventh day, and for any subsequent removals, services must be provided to the extent determined necessary, while the removal continues.

Further, within 10 business days after removing a child with a disability for more than 10 cumulative school days in a school year, the school district must convene an IEP team meeting to develop a behavioral assessment plan if the district has not already conducted a functional behavioral assessment and implemented a behavioral intervention plan for the child.

If the IEP team concludes that the child's behavior was not a manifestation of the child's disability, the child can be disciplined in the same manner as nondisabled children, except that appropriate educational services must be provided. This means that if nondisabled children are long-term suspended or expelled for a particular violation of school rules, the child with disabilities may also be long-term suspended or expelled.

Discipline for Weapon and Drug Offenses

School authorities can also unilaterally remove a disabled child from their regular placement for up to 45 days at a time if the child has brought a weapon to school or to a school function, or knowingly possessed or used illegal drugs or sold or solicited the sale of controlled substances while at school or a school function. In addition, if school officials believe that a child with a disability is substantially likely to injure himself or others in the child's regular placement, they can ask an impartial hearing officer to order that the child be removed to an interim alternative educational setting for a period of up to 45 days.

If at the end of an interim alternative educational placement of up to 45 days, school officials believe that it would be dangerous to return the child to the regular placement because the child would be substantially likely to injure himself or others in that placement, they can ask an impartial hearing officer to order that the child remain in an interim alternative educational setting for an additional 45 days. If necessary, school officials can also request subsequent extensions of these interim alternative educational settings for up to 45 days at a time if school officials continue to believe that the child would be substantially likely to injure himself or others if returned to his or her regular placement.

Additionally, at any time, school officials may seek to obtain a court order to remove a child with a disability from school or to change a child's current educational placement if they believe that maintaining the child in the current educational placement is substantially likely to result in injury to the child or others.

CHAPTER 5:
KEEPING YOUR CHILD'S SCHOOL RECORDS CONFIDENTIAL

IN GENERAL

Schools maintain records of a student's academic and personal progress from kindergarten through graduation which include, among other things, grades, progress reports, psychological reports, and teacher evaluations. As the parent of a child with special needs, the importance of maintaining the privacy of your child's records is paramount.

The records of special needs children as they go through the educational system can be voluminous, considering the extent of testing that may take place, as well as the medical and psychological reports, IEPs, evaluations, and other documentation concerning your child and his or her developmental struggles and progress.

Certainly, unauthorized persons should not have access to these private and sensitive records. As discussed below, it is your right under the law to make sure these records remain confidential.

THE FAMILY EDUCATIONAL RIGHTS AND PRIVACY ACT OF 1974

Under the Family Educational Rights and Privacy Act of 1974 (FERPA), schools that receive any federal funding must make student records available for viewing by parents and legal guardians, and by the students themselves provided they are age 18 or older. In some states the age is less than 18. For example, in Delaware and Massachusetts, the age is 14.

The purpose of FERPA is to establish requirements for the protection of privacy of parents and students. An educational agency or institution must give full rights under the Act to either parent, unless the agency or institution has been provided with evidence that there is a court order, state statute, or legally binding document relating to such matters as divorce, separation, or custody that specifically revokes these rights.

The educational agency or institution, or SEA or its component, must comply with a request for access to records within a reasonable period of time, but not more than 45 days after it has received the request.

CONSENT

A parent or eligible student must provide a signed and dated written consent before an educational agency or institution will disclose personally identifiable information from the student's education records. The written consent must:

1. Specify the records that may be disclosed;

2. State the purpose of the disclosure; and

3. Identify the party or class of parties to whom the disclosure may be made.

There are people other than the student and his or her parents who may wish to view the student's records. Although the level of protection of privacy varies from state to state, schools generally have the right to release information to teachers and school officials who have a "legitimate educational interest" in the records. This may occur, e.g, if the student transfers out of the district. Despite the written consent requirement, a school may be allowed to release a student record without obtaining permission in emergency situations where the information is necessary to protect the student's health and safety, or the health and safety of the other students.

AMENDING EDUCATION RECORDS

Inaccurate or irrelevant information contained in a student's record, such as subjective remarks by teachers, may be changed or deleted from the record upon request. If a parent or eligible student believes the education records relating to the student contain information that is inaccurate, misleading, or in violation of the student's rights of privacy, he or she may ask the educational agency or institution to amend the record.

The educational agency or institution shall decide whether to amend the record as requested within a reasonable time after the agency or institution receives the request. If the educational agency or institution decides not to amend the record as requested, it shall inform the parent or eligible student of its decision and of his or her right to a hearing.

If it is determined that there is to be no change to the record, the student and his or her parents can request that a statement be added to the record which expresses disagreement with the information. The statement becomes a permanent part of the student's record and must be released any time there is a request for the record.

PSYCHIATRIC RECORDS

There are some records which a student is not able to access, including psychiatric reports and other non-educational records possessed by a counselor, doctor, or social worker. The parents are permitted to view these files. Schools must respond to any requests for the release of files within 45 days.

SUBPOENAS

If a student's school records are subpoenaed by a court order, the school must notify the child's parents before releasing the records. In some states, the school superintendent is the only one permitted to release this information. Nevertheless, the school is not permitted to release the student's records without getting the parents' permission, unless there is an emergency situation.

FEES

An educational agency or institution may charge a fee for a copy of an education record which is made for the parent or eligible student. However, an educational agency or institution may not charge a fee to search for or to retrieve the education records of a student.

LIMITATIONS

If the education records of a student contain information on more than one student, the parent or eligible student may inspect and review or be informed of only the specific information about that student.

In addition, a postsecondary institution does not have to permit a student to inspect and review education records that are financial records, including any information those records contain, of the student's parents; or certain confidential letters and statements of recommendation placed in the education records of the student.

THE COMPLAINT PROCEDURE

A parent or eligible student may file a written complaint regarding any alleged violations of the Act. The complaints are filed with the Family

Policy Compliance Office, U.S. Department of Education, Washington, D.C. 20202-4605.

The complaint filed must contain specific allegations of fact giving reasonable cause to believe that a violation of the Act has occurred. The complaint must be submitted to the Office within 180 days of the date of the alleged violation or of the date that the complainant knew or reasonably should have known of the alleged violation. Under certain circumstances, the Office may extend the time limit.

The Office will notify the complainant if it does not initiate an investigation of a complaint because the complaint fails to meet the requirements. If the complaint is accepted, the Office investigates to determine whether the educational agency or institution has failed to comply with the provisions of the Act.

The Office will notify the complainant and the educational agency or institution in writing if it initiates an investigation of the complaint. The notice to the educational agency or institution generally includes the substance of the alleged violation; and requests the agency or institution to submit a written response to the complaint.

Once the Office reviews the complaint and response, it may permit the parties to submit further written or oral arguments or information. Following its investigation, the Office will provide the complainant and the educational agency or institution written notice of its findings and the basis for its findings.

If the Office finds that the educational agency or institution has not complied with the Act, the notice will:

> 1. Include a statement of the specific steps that the agency or institution must take to comply; and
>
> 2. Provide a reasonable period of time, given all of the circumstances of the case, during which the educational agency or institution may comply voluntarily.

HEARINGS

An educational agency or institution shall give a parent or eligible student, on request, an opportunity for a hearing to challenge the content of the student's education records on the grounds that the information contained in the education records is inaccurate, misleading, or in violation of the privacy rights of the student.

The hearing must meet, at a minimum, the following requirements:

1. The educational agency or institution shall hold the hearing within a reasonable time after it has received the request for the hearing from the parent or eligible student.

2. The educational agency or institution shall give the parent or eligible student notice of the date, time, and place, reasonably in advance of the hearing.

3. The hearing may be conducted by any individual, including an official of the educational agency or institution, who does not have a direct interest in the outcome of the hearing.

4. The educational agency or institution shall give the parent or eligible student a full and fair opportunity to present evidence relevant to the issues raised. The parent or eligible student may, at their own expense, be assisted or represented by one or more individuals of his or her own choice, including an attorney.

5. The educational agency or institution shall make its decision in writing within a reasonable period of time after the hearing.

6. The decision must be based solely on the evidence presented at the hearing.

If, as a result of the hearing, the educational agency or institution decides that the information is inaccurate, misleading, or otherwise in violation of the privacy rights of the student, it shall:

1. Amend the record accordingly; and

2. Inform the parent or eligible student of the amendment in writing.

If, as a result of the hearing, the educational agency or institution decides that the information in the education record is not inaccurate, misleading, or otherwise in violation of the privacy rights of the student, it shall inform the parent or eligible student of the right to place a statement in the record commenting on the contested information

in the record or stating why he or she disagrees with the decision of the agency or institution, or both.

If an educational agency or institution places a statement in the education records of a student, the agency or institution shall:

1. Maintain the statement with the contested part of the record for as long as the record is maintained; and

2. Disclose the statement whenever it discloses the portion of the record to which the statement relates.

CHAPTER 6:
HOME SCHOOLING YOUR CHILD

IN GENERAL

You may feel that your child would be better off being taught at home rather than in a school setting because you can give your child much needed one on one attention. While state education laws may vary, this chapter provides a general overview of typical state home schooling procedures and requirements, including those provisions relating to home instruction of the disabled child.

Because state laws may vary, the reader is advised to check the education law of his or her own state to determine the specific requirements of home schooling in their jurisdiction.

YOUR RIGHT TO HOME SCHOOL YOUR CHILD

In general, you are not required to register your child in public school if you plan to provide home instruction, however, if requested by the school district, you must prove that your child resides within the school district and is of compulsory education age.

The school district may request to meet with you to discuss the process of home schooling, however, they may not deny you the right to home instruct your child, and you may decline the school district's request for a meeting.

If you decide to enroll your child in public school after a period of home instruction, school officials will determine the appropriate grade placement of the student, and will award credit on the basis of assessment or evidence that the student has successfully completed the course work.

HOME SCHOOLING YOUR CHALLENGED CHILD

Parents of a child with special needs may also choose to home school their child, and the school district is required to provide special education services to any student who is identified as having a disability, in accordance with the child's Individualized Education Program (IEP). The school district has the obligation to offer all the services contained in the student's IEP.

In addition, the school district is required to provide transportation in order for the child to receive services, to the extent necessary to enable the student to benefit from the instruction. The need for special transportation must be addressed in the student's IEP.

Generally, special education services would be delivered at the public school. However, the district and the parents may agree to have services delivered off-site, e.g. at a library. In addition, services may be provided in the child's home if the school district and parents agree that this is the most convenient and appropriate location.

Given the nature of home instruction, a parent may assume the responsibility for providing some of the needed services outlined in the child's IEP, and may choose to have any other IEP specified services provided by the school district. However, the child's Individualize Home Instruction Plan (IHIP) should include the equivalent services listed in the IEP. As home instruction is, by its very nature, individualized and flexible, parents may provide for the needs of their children in different ways than those contained in the IEP.

Alternative evaluation measures provided in the student's IEP may be used. If the student does not have an IEP, a standardized test or a narrative evaluation, must be used, as further discussed below.

Although a school district is not generally obligated to provide textbooks and other materials to children instructed at home, the school district must provide a student with a disability who receives special education in accordance with an approved IEP with any specialized instructional materials necessary to enable the child to benefit from special education.

COURSE CURRICULUM

While the subjects required by the state education law must be taught, the course content may differ. Home instruction must include instruction in the English language, however, instruction in a foreign language is not generally required. Parents are required to provide health education at all grade levels, including instruction relating to alcohol, tobacco and drug abuse; and age appropriate instruction concerning the nature, methods of transmission and methods of prevention of the acquired immune deficiency syndrome (AIDS).

Parents may include instruction on human sexuality and family planning as part of their children's health education, but are not required to do so. In addition, home schooled students are usually required to have a physical education program with activities similar to those established for students in the public school.

Parents must submit the IHIP so that the school district can make an objective determination of substantial equivalence between the public school program and the home instruction program. A home instruction program that adheres to the standards of established regulations should be deemed to be substantially equivalent.

The school district is obligated to notify parents that the IHIP is in compliance. If the school district finds that the home instruction program is not in compliance, the parents may appeal a determination of noncompliance by the board to the Commissioner of Education within 30 days of receiving notice of the determination.

The IHIP must include for each of the required courses either a list of syllabi, curriculum materials and textbooks to be used or a plan of instruction to be followed. A different alternative may be used for different subjects. While a list of textbooks may be submitted, it is reasonable for the district to require more than the name, publisher, copyright date and author's name if the district is not familiar with the textbook's content.

If the district requests additional information beyond the list of textbooks, the parents may, at their option, submit either a written scope and sequence describing the text or a copy of the text for the district's review.

The purpose of the review is not to compare the text with those used by the district, but rather to insure that the parent is providing the mandated subjects for the grade level in question, and to provide the district with more complete information to assist its review of quarterly reports and annual assessments. Instruction should be geared to the level appropriate to the student's needs and previous level of achievement.

The total number of hours of instruction per quarter must be documented on the quarterly report. It is recommended that, in the secondary grades, hours per subject be included in each quarterly report.

EVALUATION

Parents should inform the school district of their choice of a standardized test or alternative evaluation method. It is recommended that parents provide this information to the school district by the end of the third quarterly reporting period. Any state tests designed to evaluate individual student achievement are acceptable. If the parent chooses to use a test that is not used in the public schools of the school district, the district, upon request of the parent, could order the test. The parent would, however, pay for the cost of obtaining the test.

If the parents are having the student tested at the public school, the testing should be done at the time of the school's own testing program, unless a mutually agreeable alternative is reached. The school district should give the parents several weeks' notice of the dates for this testing. If the parents are having the student tested at another location, the school district is required to review and consent to the parents' selection of the test administrator. A parent may administer a standardized test or prepare a written narrative of assessment with the consent of the superintendent.

If parents do not submit an evaluation to the district, despite requests for this information, the district should notify parents by registered mail that the evaluation is due and set a reasonable date for its submission. If the information is not forthcoming, the district is without evidence that instruction has been taking place. In that case, the district would be obligated to report the case to the proper authorities as a case of suspected educational neglect.

PROBATION

A home instruction program may be placed on probation if it does not comply with the school district's requirements, or if the child has not made adequate academic progress. Normally, if a school district requests a home visit, the parent is not required to consent. However, if a home instruction program is placed on probation, the school district may require home visits, with prior notice.

If more than one child is home schooled, the fact that the program for one child is placed on probation does not generally result in probation for the other child's home instruction program. Each child's achievement is evaluated separately.

HOME SCHOOL TEACHER

In general, the law does not require any specific credentials for the person who will be providing home instruction. Therefore, you can be your child's teacher. In addition, you may hire a tutor to provide instruction for all or a part of the home instruction program.

Although parents who home school their children may be allowed to arrange for group instruction in certain limited subjects, they cannot do so for the majority of the home instruction program. Parents who organize group instruction for the majority of the program are deemed to be operating a nonpublic school and are no longer considered to be home schooling their children.

HOME SCHOOL CALENDAR

Home instruction usually begins at the beginning of the normal school year, and is given during the days and times that school is normally in session. Nevertheless, home schooling does provide a certain degree of flexibility. For example, you may choose to provide instruction during evenings or weekends. Nevertheless, the total amount of instructional time must be comparable to the public school requirements.

If home instruction begins after the start of the school year, the parents must file a letter of intent to home school within 14 days of beginning home instruction within the district. Within 10 business days of receiving the letter of intent, the district must furnish the parent with a copy of the regulations and an IHIP form for each child.

Within 4 weeks of receiving the IHIP form, the parent must submit the completed form to the district. Within 10 business days of receiving the IHIP, the district must notify the parent whether it complies with the requirements of the regulations or give written notice of any deficiency.

Within 15 days of receiving a notice of deficiency, the parent must submit a revised IHIP which corrects the deficiencies. Within 15 days of receiving the revised IHIP, the district must notify the parent as to whether it complies with the regulations.

MISCELLANEOUS PROVISIONS

Immunizations

Students who are home schooled are generally not required to submit proof of immunization unlike children who are admitted to public school. However, if the child participates in testing or other activities on school premises, he or she may be required to produce proof of immunization otherwise the child may be denied access to school facilities.

Services and Supplies

A school district is not required to furnish health services to students who are home schooled, nor is the district required to provide remedial programs for these students. However, summer school programs are usually open to all residents of the district, whether or not home schooled.

A school district is not generally obligated to loan a home schooled student books and supplies, however, the district may offer to loan these materials to the extent available.

Recordkeeping

Parents who home school their children are required to keep attendance records. They should also keep evidence of their home instruction program, and their children's achievement. In addition, copies of any correspondence between the parent and the school district should be maintained in the file.

Extracurricular Activities

Depending on board of education policy, a child who is home schooled may be able to participate in intramural or other school-sponsored activities, such as clubs, band, etc. In addition, students who are home schooled may be able to use school facilities, such as the library or gym.

COLLEGE ADMISSION

A home schooled student does not receive a local or Regents high school diploma. High school diplomas can only be awarded to students who are enrolled in a registered secondary school and who have completed all program requirements set by the Regents, the school or the district. This may present an obstacle to the home schooled child who wants to pursue a college education.

Gaining admission to college is entirely the responsibility of home schooled students and their parents. Colleges set their own admissions requirements. The burden, therefore, is on home schooled students and their parents to seek and obtain information on the admissions requirements of the colleges of their choice.

The burden is also on home schooled students and their parents to convince colleges to accept them. Because of this, home schooled students and their parents should compile a portfolio of the child's work, demonstrating its breadth and depth, to support the college admission application.

For example, if a home schooled child has taken Regents exams at the pubic school of residence, he or she can request the public school district to produce, on school letterhead, a list of the exams taken, the date on which they were taken, and the score the child earned.

In addition, if the child has completed a program of home instruction in compliance with the education law regulations, the child can request that the superintendent of schools of the public school district of residence attest to this, in writing, on district letterhead. The school district may, but is under no obligation to, attest to this.

Home schooled students can also take the GED exam, when they have reached eligibility to do so, and can take the Scholastic Aptitude Test (SAT) and any other standardized tests used for college admissions purposes. Home schooled students should contact their public school district about arrangements for taking the Scholastic Aptitude Test and achievement examinations offered by the College Board or the American College Testing Service.

CHAPTER 7:
OBTAINING FINANCIAL AND HEALTH BENEFITS FOR YOUR CHILD

IN GENERAL

Your special needs child may be eligible to receive benefits under various federal and state programs. The Social Security Administration (SSA) administers the two main programs that provide financial and health benefits to disabled children: Supplemental Security Income (SSI) and Medicaid. In addition, there are other benefit programs designed to meet the needs of these children.

SUPPLEMENTAL SECURITY INCOME (SSI)

The Supplemental Security Income (SSI) program is a federal welfare program for adults and children who are disabled or blind, and people aged 65 and over with low income and few financial resources. The SSI program was originally established for persons who had become disabled and therefore could no longer work.

SSI is a cash assistance program for persons who meet both a disability and income requirement. SSI provides a basic payment for an eligible individual. People who qualify for SSI receive a check each month. The amount of benefit may vary depending on the recipient's state of residence and level of income.

Eligibility for SSI/SSDI

Part B is a program designed to provide disabled children with the same monetary benefit. Under the SSI program, a child from birth to age 18 may receive monthly payments based on disability or blindness if:

    1. He or she has an impairment or combination of impairments that meets the definition of disability for children—i.e., the child has a

physical or mental condition, or a combination of conditions, that results in "marked and severe functional limitations." This means that the condition(s) very seriously limits his or her activities; and

2. The income and resources of the parents and the child are within the allowed limits.

Under the Social Security Disability Insurance (SSDI) program, an adult child—a person age 18 or older—may receive monthly benefits based on disability or blindness if:

1. He or she has an impairment or combination of impairments that meets the definition of disability for adults; and

2. The disability began before age 22; and

3. The adult child's parent worked long enough to be insured under Social Security and is receiving retirement or disability benefits or is deceased.

Under both the SSI and SSDI programs, the child must not be doing any "substantial" work, and must have a medical condition that has lasted or is expected to last for at least 1 year, or is expected to result in death.

Many states rely on the Children with Special Health Care Needs programs in their states to assist in determining disability, including the use of pediatricians to review charts and make recommendations.

Although SSI is a federal program, some states supplement the national payments and have established higher SSI rates and allow higher income limits than others. Unlike the "income" limits, however, the SSI "asset" limits do not vary among the states.

The reader is advised to check the SSI eligibility criteria of their own jurisdiction.

If your child qualifies for SSI benefits, he or she is also automatically entitled to health care coverage under the Medicaid program. You can apply for SSI and Medicaid benefits on behalf of your child by completing forms provided by your local welfare office, department of social services or Social Security Administration (SSA) office. If the application is approved, your child will be paid benefits based on the date the application was filed.

Redetermination

The SSA reviews every SSI case from time to time to make sure those who are receiving checks are still eligible and entitled to receive benefits. Thus, you may be periodically required to prove that your child is still disabled. The review also determines if the individuals are receiving the correct amounts. This process is called "redetermination."

To decide whether your child is disabled, the SSA looks at medical and other information about the child's condition, and considers how the condition affects his or her daily activities. In making this determination, the SSA considers the following:

1. What activities is your child not able to do, or is limited in doing?

2. What kind of and how much extra help does your child need to perform age-appropriate activities—for example, special classes at school, medical equipment?

3. Do the effects of treatment interfere with your child's day-to-day activities?

If you receive a notice advising you that your child's disability status will be reviewed, you should provide the SSA with all of the records and reports you have that demonstrates your child's disability status. You should also provide the SSA with the names and addresses of all professionals who have records concerning your child's disability, including hospitals, schools, doctors' offices, therapists' offices, social service agencies, and mental health agencies.

Your Right to Appeal

If your child's application for SSI benefits is not approved, or benefits are ceased after a redetermination proceeding, you can appeal the SSA's decision. You have 60 days to submit a written request for reconsideration. The request should be sent to the local Social Security district office, and should state the reasons why you disagree with the determination. Depending on the nature of the issue, either a case review, a formal conference or a hearing may follow.

To prepare for the reconsideration appeal, you should gather all of your child's medical records and school records, such as grades, attendance, and IEP's if your child is in a special education program. In addition, ask each of your child's doctors, psychiatrists, therapists, special education teachers, and social workers to complete the detailed questionnaire about your child's disability.

Send your child's medical and school records and completed questionnaires to Social Security as soon as possible after you receive them. Keep copies of whatever you give to Social Security and take the copies to any future meetings with Social Security, such as the Reconsideration Conference.

If your child has not been to his or her doctor or therapist recently, begin treatment with the doctor or therapist immediately so that you can show that your child still has the disability you are claiming.

Your child will continue to receive SSI benefits during the appeal process if you appeal within 10 days of the date listed on the notice. Even if it takes months for Social Security to decide whether your child still qualifies for SSI, you will continue to receive checks if the appeal is filed within 10 days.

Although appeals can be filed after the 10-day deadline has passed, if you don't have a good reason for the delay, your child will not receive SSI benefits during the appeal process.

If Social Security rules that your child is not disabled, you may be asked to pay back the money you received while the appeal was pending. However, you may ask Social Security to forgive the debt. Only parents who can afford to repay the money without hardship, or parents whose child is obviously not disabled, are denied waivers of the repayment requirement.

During the appeal process, the SSA will review all of your evidence and make a determination. You can also request a reconsideration hearing where you and your child will have an opportunity to speak with the person who will be deciding your appeal.

If you lose the reconsideration appeal, you should file an application for the next level of appeal—a Request for a Hearing—within 60 days of the date on the denial notice. While you are waiting for a hearing date, make sure your child continues to get all necessary medical treatment. As you gather more evidence, provide copies to the SSA. You should also consult an attorney for possible representation at your hearing.

A directory of attorneys who represent parents of children with disabilities is set forth at Appendix 10.

Dedicated Accounts

When an eligible child under age 18, who has a representative payee, is eligible for certain large past due payments covering more than six months of benefits, these payments must be paid directly into a separate account in a financial institution known as a dedicated account.

The representative payee or the child may use the funds in a dedicated account only for certain expenses, primarily those related to the child's disability. The dedicated account must be maintained separately from any other savings or checking account set up for your child.

MEDICAID

Medicaid is jointly financed and administered by the federal and state governments as the primary source of health care coverage for blind, disabled, and low-income individuals. As set forth above, if your child qualifies for SSI benefits, he or she is automatically eligible for Medicaid benefits.

Each state has its own rules concerning eligibility and coverage, which may be complex, therefore, the reader is advised to check the law of his or her own jurisdiction for specific rules.

In general, to be eligible for Medicaid, your child must fit into a Medicaid eligibility category. Once it is determined that your child fits into a Medicaid eligible category, the household's financial situation is examined. Your income and resources are analyzed to determine your "countable" income and resources. Your countable income is then compared to the income guideline set by the state—i.e., the maximum amount of income a person can have and still be eligible for Medicaid.

If the household income is less than or equal to the guideline, the child is considered income-eligible. A similar analysis is made of the household resources. If it is determined that the child is both income-eligible and resource-eligible, he or she is considered qualified for Medicaid benefits.

Although states have discretion in setting their own income and resources guidelines, in order to qualify for federal funds, the federal government requires the states to provide Medicaid coverage under certain circumstances to specified groups, including SSI recipients, which generally include blind, disabled, and needy elderly individuals.

The 1915 Katie Beckett Medicaid Waiver

Medicaid Waivers are state-run programs that use federal and state funds to pay for health care for people with certain health conditions. For example, the 1915 Katie Beckett waiver permits a family with a special needs child to receive Medicaid in order to have health care services and supports that keep their child at home, rather than in a hospital or institution.

Medically Needy Programs

Children whose parents' income exceeds the income eligibility requirements may still qualify for Medicaid benefits under a state's medically needy program. A medically needy program permits a family whose child has incurred high medical bills to apply those bills to their household income in order to reduce their income to a level where their child can then qualify for Medicaid. Nevertheless, the child must still meet the SSA disability determination to be eligible for this program.

The Early and Periodic Screening, Diagnostic, and Treatment Program (EPSDT)

The Early and Periodic Screening, Diagnostic, and Treatment (EPSDT) program is Medicaid's comprehensive and preventive child health program for individuals under the age of 21. EPSDT includes periodic screening, vision, dental, and hearing services. In addition, Section 1905(a) of the Social Security Act requires that any medically necessary health care service listed in the statute be provided to an EPSDT recipient, even if the service is not available under the State's Medicaid plan to the rest of the Medicaid population.

EPSDT services include:

1. Podiatrist Services
2. Optometrist Services
3. Chiropractic Services
4. Other Practitioner Services
5. Private Duty Nursing
6. Clinic Services
7. Skilled Nursing Facility
8. Emergency Hospital Services
9. Personal Care Services
10. Transportation
11. Case Management
12. Hospice Services
13. Diagnostic Services
14. Preventive Services
15. Rehabilitative Services
16. Intermediate Care Facilities
17. ICF for the Mentally Retarded
18. Inpatient Psychiatric Services
19. Christian Science Nurses/sanatoria

20. Physical Therapy
21. Occupational Therapy
22. Speech-Language-Hearing Services
23. Prescribed Drugs
24. Prosthetic devices
25. Eyeglasses

YOUR CHILD'S EARNINGS

Many children want to work at a part-time job at some point, therefore, it is important to understand how a child's earnings can affect his or her eligibility for benefits.

The SSA does not count most of a child's earnings when figuring the SSI payment, and count even less of a child's earnings if the child is a student. The SSA also subtracts the cost of certain items and services that a child needs to work from his or her earnings in figuring the SSI payment.

If your child is age 15 or older, he or she can establish a Plan to Achieve Self-Support (PASS). With a PASS, a child can set aside income for a work goal. The SSA does not count this income in figuring the SSI payment.

A child's Medicaid coverage can continue even if his or her earnings are high enough to stop SSI payments, as long as the earnings are under a certain amount.

STATE CHILDREN'S HEALTH INSURANCE PROGRAM (SCHIP)

Children may be able to get health insurance from the State Children's Health Insurance Program (SCHIP) even if they do not get SSI. SCHIP provides health insurance to children from working families with incomes too high to get Medicaid, but who cannot afford private health insurance. SCHIP provides insurance for prescription drugs and for vision, hearing and mental health services in all 50 states and the District of Columbia.

TITLE V OF THE SOCIAL SECURITY ACT

Title V of the Social Security Act provides the basis for public health programs funded by the federal government. It is administered by the Department of Health and Human Services, under the Health Resources and Services Administration (HRSA) through the Maternal and

Child Health Bureau (MCHB). The MCHB administers seven major programs:

1. The Maternal and Child Health Services Block Grant
2. The Healthy Start Initiative
3. Emergency Medical Services for Children Program
4. The Abstinence Education Program
5. Traumatic Brain Injury
6. Universal Newborn Hearing Screening
7. Poison Control Centers Program

Like Medicaid (Title XIX), Title V is a federal/state-matching program. For every $4 provided by the federal government, $3 must be matched through state funds. The Division of Services for Children with Special Health Care Needs has two branches: (1) the Integrated Services Branch; and (2) The Genetics Services Branch.

The Integrated Services Branch

The Integrated Services Branch promotes leadership and support for the development and implementation of innovative, replicable models of community-based care for children with special health care needs in six program areas:

1. Medical Home
2. Financing/Managed Care
3. Family/Professional Partnership/Cultural Competence
4. Healthy and Ready to Work
5. Community Integrated Services
6. Universal Newborn Hearing and Screening

The Genetics Services Branch

The Genetics Services Branch facilitates the early identification of children with genetic conditions and works to increase public and professional awareness of how genetic diseases affect health in order to create a more responsive system of care. It administers five program areas:

1. Newborn Screening
2. Emerging Issues in Genetics
3. Improving Genetic Literacy
4. Health Professionals' Training

5. Hemophilia and Other Chronic Diseases

Title V programs usually provide care coordination services although some states provide clinical services. These services are usually provided in collaboration with Medicaid and private insurance. Under the law, Title V can bill patients/families for services provided using a sliding fee scale based on income. Most services are free of charge, unless the patient has Medicaid or private insurance. There is a recent requirement that applicants denied SSI be referred to Title V.

States choose the types of services they provide and define who is eligible for those services. When applying for funding, states must submit documentation to the MCHB detailing how many children have special health care needs and how they will receive services.

CHAPTER 8:
DISABILITY LEGISLATION

CASE LAW AND LEGISLATIVE DEVELOPMENTS

Discrimination in the public education of disabled children was commonplace in the United States until the early 1970s, when litigation and legislation guaranteed the disabled child's right to an education. Following are landmark cases which helped to establish and protect the disabled child's right to an education.

Brown v. Board of Education

In 1954, the U.S. Supreme Court handed down its decision in *Brown v. Board of Education*, 347 U.S. 483 (1954). *Brown* was a landmark civil rights case which established the principle that all children must be guaranteed an equal educational opportunity. In **Brown**, the Court found that segregated public schools were inherently unequal and deprived African-American children of equal protection under the law.

The Court stated that "it is doubtful that any child may reasonably be expected to succeed in life if he is denied the opportunity of an education . . . [S]uch an opportunity, where the state has undertaken to provide it, is a right which must be made available to all on equal terms."

Shortly after *Brown* was decided, parents of disabled children started to file lawsuits against their school districts for segregating children with disabilities, arguing that exclusion of disabled children was also discrimination.

Mills v. Board of Education of District of Columbia

In 1972, another important decision was made in *Mills v. Board of Education of District of Columbia*, 348 F. Supp. 866 (D. DC 1972). *Mills* involved the practice of suspending, expelling and excluding "exceptional" children from the District of Columbia public schools. The Court found that the District of Columbia failed to provide publicly supported education and training to plaintiffs and other "'exceptional" children and members of their class, and excluded, suspended, reassigned, and transferred "exceptional" children from regular public school classes without affording them due process of law.

Board of Education v. Rowley

In *Board of Education v. Rowley*, 458 U.S. 176 (1982), the U.S. Supreme Court issued its first decision in a special education discrimination case. The reader is advised to refer to this decision insofar as the Court sets forth a comprehensive analysis of the evolution of special education law.

THE REHABILITATION ACT OF 1973

The Rehabilitation Act of 1973 was enacted to protect the rights of disabled persons, in general. It is the predecessor of the Americans with Disabilities Act (ADA), and served as a model for drafters of the ADA. Section 504 was intended to prevent intentional or unintentional discrimination against persons with disabilities, persons who are believed to have disabilities, or family members of persons with disabilities.

Section 504 of the Rehabilitation Act provides that qualified disabled individuals cannot be excluded from, denied the benefits of, or be subjected to discrimination under any program or activity that receives Federal financial assistance solely by reason of their handicap.

Agencies that provide Federal financial assistance also have Section 504 regulations covering entities that receive Federal aid. Because all public schools receive some type of federal assistance, Section 504 applies to public educational institutions. For educational institutions, the term "program or activity" includes any of the operations of a State educational agency (SEA) and local educational agency (LEA) receiving federal funds regardless of whether the specific program or activity involved is a direct recipient of the federal funds.

Further, the definition of a disability under Section 504 is much broader than the definition under the IDEA, which is discussed below. Thus, all children covered under the IDEA would be covered under Section 504, whereas not all children covered under Section 504 would be covered under the IDEA.

Section 504 protects all persons with a disability who:

1. Have a physical or mental impairment which substantially limits one or more major life activities;

2. Have a record of such an impairment; or

3. Are regarded as having such an impairment.

Section 504 regulations further define a "physical or mental impairment" as any physiological disorder or condition, cosmetic disfigurement or anatomical loss affecting one or more of the following body systems: (i) neurological, (ii) musculoskeletal, (iii) special sense organs, (iv) respiratory including speech organs, (v) cardiovascular, (vi) reproductive, digestive, (vii) genito-urinary, hemic and lymphatic, (viii) skin or endocrine; or (ix) any mental or psychological disorder such as mental retardation, organic brain syndrome, emotional or mental illness and specific learning disabilities.

In order to be covered under Section 504, the disabled person's physical or mental impairment must have a substantial limitation on one or more major life activities, such as seeing, hearing, learning, etc. As it applies to disabled children, the issue is whether the child's impairment substantially limits his or her ability to learn.

Section 504 places responsibility on the schools to identify students with disabilities. Each school must undertake an annual investigation to identify every qualified individual with a disability residing in the school's jurisdiction who is not receiving a public education.

Section 504 requires that parents receive notice of actions regarding the identification, evaluation and placement of their children. The notice does not need to be in writing, although many districts do provide written notice so they can document the event if they are challenged. However, unlike the IDEA, there is no consent requirement under Section 504.

Selected provisions of Section 504 of the Rehabilitation Act of 1973 are set forth at Appendix 11.

THE EDUCATION FOR ALL HANDICAPPED CHILDREN ACT OF 1975 (EAHCA)

The Education for All Handicapped Children Act (EAHCA), which was enacted in 1975, established the disabled child's right to a "free appropriate public education." The EAHCA was the predecessor to the Individuals with Disabilities Education Act (IDEA), the primary law dealing with the education of disabled children.

Under the Act, the "free appropriate public education" is to be undertaken in the least restrictive environment appropriate to the student's individual needs. The desire to educate the disabled child in a setting which includes non-disabled children—a process known as "mainstreaming"—is emphasized, to the extent possible. The child's placement must also be in a setting which is as close to the child's home as available and appropriate, preferably in the school the child would be attending if he or she was not disabled.

DISABILITY LEGISLATION

Under the EAHCA, a substantial financial commitment was made by the federal government to educate learning disabled students. The Act also established a process by which State and local educational agencies may be held accountable for providing educational services for all handicapped children. Since the Act was enacted, the term "handicapped" has been replaced with the term "disabled."

THE HANDICAPPED CHILDREN'S PROTECTION ACT OF 1986

In 1986, Congress strengthened the Act by passing The Handicapped Children's Protection Act (HCPA). The HCPA amended the EAHCA by awarding attorney's fees and costs to parents who are successful in litigation.

THE INDIVIDUALS WITH DISABILITIES EDUCATION ACT (IDEA)

The Individuals with Disabilities Education Act (IDEA) expanded upon and strengthened the provisions contained in its predecessor, the Education for All Handicapped Children Act, which was reauthorized in 1990 and retitled. The IDEA is the most significant piece of legislation affecting the educational rights of disabled children.

Selected provisions of the Individuals with Disabilities Education Act are set forth at Appendix 12.

Before the IDEA was implemented in 1975 as the EAHCA, approximately 1 million disabled children were excluded from schools, and thousands more were denied appropriate services. The IDEA has changed the lives of many disabled children, who are finishing high school and attending college in unprecedented numbers.

The Individuals with Disabilities Education Act (IDEA) requires public schools to locate and identify children with disabilities who may be in need of specialized education. The IDEA is divided into four parts:

Part A: General Provisions, Definitions and Other Issues

Part A discusses the purpose of the special education law and includes definitions of terms that are used in the statute.

Part B: Assistance for Education of All Children with Disabilities

Part B includes funding, state plans, evaluations, eligibility, due process, discipline and other areas relating to direct services.

Part C: Infants and Toddlers with Disabilities

Part C refers to infants and children with disabilities, and defines an "at-risk infant or toddler" as an individual under 3 years of age who would be at risk of experiencing a substantial developmental delay if early intervention services were not provided.

Part D: National Activities to Improve Education of Children with Disabilities

Part D focuses on the need to improve special education programs, prepare personnel, disseminate information, supporting research, and apply research findings to education.

Covered Persons

Under the IDEA, a child with a disability is defined as a child:

(i) with mental retardation; hearing impairments including deafness; speech or language impairments; visual impairments, including blindness; serious emotional disturbance; orthopedic impairments; autism; traumatic brain injury; or other health impairments, or specific learning disabilities; and

(ii) who, by reason thereof, needs special education and related services.

The IDEA defines special education as specially designed instruction, at no cost to parents, to meet the unique needs of a child with a disability, including:

(A) instruction conducted in the classroom, in the home, in hospitals and institutions, and in other settings; and

(B) instruction in physical education.

A Free Appropriate Public Education

Equal educational opportunity to disabled children is achieved through the provision of a free appropriate public education (FAPE). Every qualified student with a disability is entitled to a free appropriate public education regardless of the nature or severity of their disability.

The Individual Education Program (IEP)

Under the IDEA, a child who is referred for evaluation undergoes comprehensive individual testing to determine whether he or she has a disability eligible for special education and related support services. If the child is deemed eligible for special education, public school systems are required to develop appropriate Individualized Education Programs (IEPs) for the child, which must be reviewed annually.

The Individualized Education Program is discussed more fully in Chapter 4 of this almanac.

DISABILITY LEGISLATION

The law mandates that particular procedures be followed in the development of the IEP. The IEP must be developed by a team of knowledgeable persons, including the child's teacher; the parents, subject to certain limited exceptions; the child, if determined appropriate; an agency representative who is qualified to provide or supervise the provision of special education; and other individuals at the parents' or agency's discretion.

If parents disagree with the proposed IEP, they can request a due process hearing and review by the state educational department. They also can appeal the state agency decision to State or Federal court.

The IDEA Amendments of 1997

In May 1997, after two years of intense analysis, discussion, legislative proposals and hearings, the U.S. House of Representatives and Senate passed legislation reauthorizing and amending the IDEA. On June 4, 1997, former President Clinton signed the bill into law. The reauthorized IDEA is called the "Individuals with Disabilities Education Act Amendments of 1997," Public Law 105-17, codified at 20 U.S.C. 1401 et seq.

The signing of the IDEA Amendments was the culmination of a process begun by the Office of Special Education and Rehabilitative Services (OSERS) in the U.S. Department of Education ("Department") in the early 1990s to review the effectiveness of the IDEA since it was first enacted in 1975 and to propose clarifications and improvements to the law in light of over two decades of experience.

Following is a summary of the IDEA Amendments of 1997 and the final regulations implementing the Amendments in 1999:

1. The least restrictive environment (LRE) requirements are maintained and strengthened in many references to educating children with disabilities. For example, children with disabilities must have access to and participate in the general education curriculum.

2. The rights of parents to be involved in educational decisions effecting their children including eligibility and placement decisions are reinforced and strengthened.

3. Challenging behavior is best approached proactively through the use of functional behavioral assessments, and positive behavior strategies, interventions and supports.

4. Children with disabilities must be included in school reform efforts as well as in state and district-wide assessments.

5. The IDEA adopted an outcome-based approach to special education; the state must establish performance goals and indicators to measure and report progress.

6. The IDEA calls on state and local agencies to engage in system-wide capacity building, linking student progress with school improvement.

The IDEA Amendments are also divided into four parts:

Part A: General Provisions

This part contains the findings and purposes of the law and the goals for the new amendments. These goals include:

1. Raising the expectations for children with disabilities and ensuring their access to the general education curriculum;

2. Strengthening the role of parents and ensuring that families have meaningful opportunities to participate in the education of their children;

3. Providing special education and related services, aids and supports in the regular classroom when appropriate; and

4. Responding to the educational needs of minority children in an increasingly diverse society.

Part A includes definitions of many of the terms used in the Act. It also clarifies the procedures regarding the U.S. Department of Education's use of policy letters and other correspondence.

Part B: Assistance for Education of All Children with Disabilities.

Part B describes the means by which the federal government will assist the states in carrying out the purposes of the Act and how the local educational agencies shall provide a free appropriate public education to students with disabilities between the ages of 3 and 21. Part B also includes the basic rights and responsibilities of children with disabilities and their parents.

Part C: Infants and Toddlers with Disabilities

Part C addresses the needs of infants and toddlers ages birth to 3 years old.

Part D: National Activities to Improve Education of Children with Disabilities

Part D authorizes discretionary programs to improve the education of children with disabilities.

DISABILITY LEGISLATION

Significant Changes

A number of significant changes were accomplished with the enactment of the IDEA Amendments, as set forth below:

Child with a Disability

The definition of a "child with a disability" was amended to add "attention deficit disorder" and "attention deficit hyperactivity disorder" to the list of conditions that can render a child eligible for special education and related services.

The regulation clarifies that for children with ADD or ADHD, the phrase "limited strength or vitality or alertness" that defines "other health impairments" includes "a child's heightened alertness to environmental stimuli that results in limited alertness with respect to the educational environment," common characteristics of many children with ADD or ADHD.

Attention Deficit Hyperactivity Disorder is more fully discussed in Chapter 2 of this almanac.

Seriously Emotionally Disturbed

The regulations restate the change in the statute that the term "seriously emotionally disturbed" is now called "emotionally disturbed." The change in this term was not intended to have any substantive or legal significance, but was intended strictly to eliminate the pejorative connotations of the word "serious."

Parent Counseling and Training

The revised regulation adds that parent counseling and training also means "helping parents to acquire the necessary skills that will allow them to support the implementation of their child's IEP or IFSP."

Transportation

The regulations state that most children with disabilities should receive the same transportation services as non-disabled children. Further, for some children with disabilities integrated transportation may be achieved by providing needed accommodations such as lifts and other equipment or adaptations on regular school transportation vehicles.

Removals and Suspensions

A new amendment to the IDEA explicitly states that the state must ensure that a free appropriate public education (FAPE) is provided to all children with disabilities between the ages of 3 and 21, including children who have been suspended or expelled from school. The revised regulation clarifies, however, that during the first ten school days in that school year for which a child with a disability is suspended or otherwise removed from his or her placement because of a violation of school conduct rules, the school district does not need to provide services to the child with a disability if the school does not provide services to non-disabled children who have been similarly removed.

After a child has been removed from his or her current placement by school personnel for cumulatively more than 10 school days in the same school year, subsequent short term removals are permissible as long as they do not constitute a change of placement.

However, for these removals beyond ten school days, services must be provided to the extent necessary to enable the child to appropriately progress in the general curriculum and appropriately advance toward the child's IEP goals. In this situation, school personnel, in consultation with the child's special education teacher, determine the extent to which services are necessary.

Graduation

The revised regulation includes longstanding Department policy that a student's right to a FAPE is terminated upon graduation with a regular high school diploma. Graduation from high school with a regular diploma is considered a change in placement and the school must give prior written notice. However, the statutory provision which requires re-evaluation before any change in the child's eligibility, does not apply when the child is graduating from high school with a regular diploma.

Advancement

The revised regulation includes the longstanding Department policy that each state must ensure that a FAPE is available to any child who needs special education and related services, even though the child is advancing from grade to grade.

The Least Restrictive Environment

The amendments maintain the same Least Restrictive Environment (LRE) standard and requirements and add that a state's funding formula must not violate these requirements. The new law further strengthens the LRE requirement by requiring in the IEP an explanation of the extent to which the child will not participate with non-disabled children in academic, non-academic and extracurricular activities.

The statute also includes a new definition for "supplementary aids and services" which includes a range of services provided in regular education classes or other settings to enable disabled children to be educated with non-disabled children to the maximum extent appropriate.

Parentally Placed Children

The new law requires parents to provide notice to the IEP team of their intent to remove the child from the public school and place their child in a private school. This notice must be provided either at the most recent IEP meeting prior to removal or in writing within 10 business days prior to removal. If the parents do not provide such notice, reimbursement of the cost of the private school may be reduced or denied.

Placement

The revised regulation states that the services provided to a child with a disability must address all of the child's identified special education and related services and must be based on educational needs and not on the child's disability category.

Assistive Technology

The revised regulation specifies that assistive technology devices and services may be considered special education, related services, or supplementary aids and services.

Assistive Technology is discussed more fully in Chapter 7 of this almanac.

Extended School Year

The revised regulation generally restates the Department's long-standing policy regarding extended school year services that such services must be provided only if a child's IEP team determines, on an individual basis, that the services are necessary for the provision of a free appropriate public education to the child. Further, an LEA may not limit extended school year services to particular categories of disability, or unilaterally limit the type, amount, or duration of those services.

Parent Participation in Eligibility and Placement Decisions

Parents are specifically included as members of the group making the decision regarding the child's eligibility for special education services and educational placement.

Reevaluations

The amendments streamline the requirements regarding the reevaluation of special education students every three years. Now, at least every three years, the IEP team must review existing evaluation data on the child, and based on that review as well as input from the parents, identify what additional information, if any, is needed to determine the following:

1. Whether the child continues to have a disability and continues to need special education and related services;

2. The child's present levels of performance and educational needs; and

3. Whether additions or modifications to the special education and related services are needed to enable the child to meet the goals set out in the IEP and to participate in the general curriculum.

If the IEP team believes that it needs more information or data to address the questions above, tests and other evaluation procedures shall be conducted in order to gather the specific information needed. If the IEP team and other qualified professionals find that no additional data is needed to determine whether the child continues to be a child with a disability, the local educational agency:

1. Shall notify the child's parents of that determination and the reasons for it, and the right of the parent to request an assessment to determine if the child continues to be a child with a disability; and

2. Shall not be required to conduct such an assessment unless requested to by the parents.

Private Education Under the Individuals With Disabilities Education Act

As the Individuals With Disabilities Education Act (IDEA) relates to private education, Part B of the Act requires states and school districts to locate, identify, and evaluate, at public expense, those students placed by their parents in private schools who are suspected of having disabilities and needing special education and related services.

School districts must also make available a "free appropriate public education" to those parentally placed students who are determined to have disabilities. A free appropriate public education is made available at a public school setting or another appropriate setting determined by the district.

The requirement to make available a free appropriate public education does not extend beyond these settings to a private school when the child with disabilities is parentally placed in that setting. However, school districts must provide parentally placed students with disabilities who are enrolled in private elementary and secondary schools a genuine opportunity for equitable participation in their special education program, and make a free appropriate public education available to each eligible disabled student if the parents return their child to the public school.

DISABILITY LEGISLATION

Even though Part B does not require that all parentally placed students with disabilities receive services, in designing how the school district will provide special education services to private school students with disabilities, consideration must be given to the needs of all of the private school students with disabilities and the full range of services under Part B.

School districts must consult with appropriate representatives of students enrolled in private schools in determining, among other matters, which parentally placed disabled students will receive benefits under the program, how the students' needs will be identified, the types of services to be offered, and the manner in which the services will be provided, including the site where the services are offered and how the services under Part B will be evaluated.

The Part B program benefits provided to parentally placed students with disabilities must be comparable in quality, scope, and opportunity for participation to the program benefits provided to public school students. The "comparable benefits" provision means that students in private schools must be given the same general types of services that public school students receive and these services must be of the same general quality.

Examples of services that could be provided to parentally placed students with disabilities under Part B include speech pathology, occupational therapy, physical therapy, consultations with the private school classroom teacher, and teacher training and professional development for private school personnel. Equipment and supplies also can be provided to private school students with disabilities on the premises of the private school.

The IDEA reaffirms the public school's obligation to afford all eligible children with disabilities a free appropriate public education in the least restrictive environment appropriate to their individual needs, and the requirement to develop an appropriate Individualized Education Program (IEP) for each child.

Individualized Education Programs are discussed more fully in Chapter 4 of this almanac.

THE FAMILY EDUCATIONAL RIGHTS AND PRIVACY ACT OF 1974

According to the Family Educational Rights and Privacy Act ("FERPA"), schools that receive any federal funding must make student records available for viewing by parents and legal guardians, and by the students themselves provided they are age 18 or older.

The Family Educational Rights and Privacy Act is more fully discussed in Chapter 5 of this almanac.

THE AMERICANS WITH DISABILITIES ACT OF 1990

The Americans with Disabilities Act (ADA) contains five titles:

1. Title I: Equal Employment Opportunity for Individuals with Disabilities—This title is designed to remove barriers that would deny qualified individuals with disabilities access to the same employment opportunities and benefits available to others without disabilities.

2. Title II: Nondiscrimination on the Basis of Disability in State and Local Government Services—This title prohibits discrimination on the basis of disability by public entities, including elementary and secondary public schools, and provides the basis for disability discrimination claims.

3. Title III: Nondiscrimination on the Basis of Disability by Public Accommodations and in Commercial Facilities—This title prohibits discrimination on the basis of disability by private entities in places of public accommodation, and requires that all new places of public accommodation and commercial facilities be designed and constructed so that they are readily accessible to, and usable by, persons with disabilities.

4. Title IV: Telecommunications—This title requires telephone companies to have developed interstate and intrastate telephone relay services in order to allow people with speech and hearing impairments who use TDDs to communicate with individuals who do not have this equipment.

5. Title V: Miscellaneous Provisions

Disability Discrimination Under Title II of the ADA

The U.S. Department of Education's Office for Civil Rights (OCR) enforces Title II in public elementary and secondary education systems and institutions, public institutions of higher education and vocational education.

Title II covers, for example, any public entertainment or lecture series a school system offers, after-school activities and social events offered by a school system, parent-teacher meetings, classroom activities, field trips or other special events, and all services provided for students or staff. Services provided by any private contractors on behalf of the school system must also comply fully with relevant provisions of Title II.

Under Title II, many of the provisions of Section 504 of the Rehabilitation Act were expanded upon. In fact, because of their similarities, both the ADA and Section 504 are administered by the Office for Civil Rights (OCR) and considered essentially identical.

Because the ADA regulations have no specific provisions regarding education programs, in interpreting the ADA, the OCR uses the standards under Section 504, except where Title II provides otherwise. The ADA statute clearly specifies, however, that unless Title II states otherwise, Title II may not be interpreted to apply a lesser degree of protection to individuals with disabilities than is provided under Section 504.

In the area of education, the federal government has stated many of the nondiscrimination requirements related to individuals with disabilities in more specific detail under Section 504 than under Title II. The reason for this difference is that the regulation issued to implement Title II was written to cover all state and local government entities regardless of their function.

On the other hand, the regulation issued under Section 504 was written to describe specific requirements applicable to public school districts, as well as certain other types of recipients of federal funds in the areas of education, health, and social services. Nevertheless, if a rule issued under Section 504 imposes a lesser standard than the ADA statute or regulation, the language in the ADA statute or regulation controls.

As it applies to disabled students, virtually every violation of Section 504 is also a violation of Title II. Thus, the OCR has stated that complaints alleging violations of one statute will automatically be investigated for violations of the other.

Title II prohibits discrimination against any "qualified individual with a disability." In addition, Title II also protects persons who, because of their association with persons who have disabilities, have been retaliated against for their participation in Title II activities.

Disabilities covered by Title II are limited to those that meet the ADA's legal definition—i.e., those that place substantial limitations on one or more of an individual's major life activities, and includes an individual:

(A) who has a physical or mental impairment that substantially limits one or more of the major life activities of such individual, i.e., those persons who *currently* have actual physical or mental impairments that substantially limit one or more major life activities;

(B) who has a record of such an impairment; or

(C) who is being regarded as having such an impairment.

The phrase "major life activities" includes but is not limited to functions such as caring for one's self, performing manual tasks, walking, seeing, hearing, speaking, breathing, learning, and working.

To be considered a disability, the impairment must significantly restrict the performance of a major life activity in comparison to most people in terms of (i) conditions under which the activity is performed; (ii) the manner in which the activity is performed; or (iii) the duration of performance possible for the individual.

The finding that an impairment poses a substantial limitation is not assumed simply because an impairment exists; it is shown by determining the impact of that impairment on a particular individual. The factors that are considered in determining whether a person's impairment substantially limits a major life activity are (i) its nature and severity; (ii) its duration; and (iii) its permanent or long-term impact or expected impact.

Persons with records of physical or mental impairments includes those who have a history or record of an impairment that substantially limits a major life activity, as well as persons who have been misclassified as having an impairment.

Persons regarded as having a disability refers to people who are not, in fact, substantially limited in any major life activity but are nevertheless perceived by others as having a disability, sometimes because of myth, fear, or stereotype.

Selected provisions of the Americans with Disabilities Act are set forth at Appendix 13.

THE IMPROVING AMERICA'S SCHOOLS ACT OF 1994

The Improving America's Schools Act (IASA) reauthorized the Elementary and Secondary Education Act (ESEA), the principal federal law affecting education from kindergarten through high school, which in turn authorizes programs to benefit educationally needy elementary and secondary students living in areas with high concentrations of children from low-income families.

THE NO CHILD LEFT BEHIND ACT

On January 8, 2002, the No Child Left Behind Act (NCLB) became law. With passage of No Child Left Behind, Congress again reauthorized the Elementary and Secondary Education Act (ESEA) and implemented

DISABILITY LEGISLATION

new programs designed to meet the educational needs of elementary and secondary students, including children with disabilities. Section 1001 of the No Child Left Behind Act sets forth its statement of purpose:

The purpose of this title is to ensure that all children have a fair, equal, and significant opportunity to obtain a high-quality education and reach, at a minimum, proficiency on challenging State academic achievement standards and state academic assessments.

This purpose can be accomplished by:

(1) ensuring that high-quality academic assessments, accountability systems, teacher preparation and training, curriculum, and instructional materials are aligned with challenging State academic standards so that students, teachers, parents, and administrators can measure progress against common expectations for student academic achievement;

(2) meeting the educational needs of low-achieving children in our Nation's highest-poverty schools, limited English proficient children, migratory children, children with disabilities, Indian children, neglected or delinquent children, and young children in need of reading assistance;

(3) closing the achievement gap between high-and low-performing children, especially the achievement gaps between minority and nonminority students, and between disadvantaged children and their more advantaged peers;

(4) holding schools, local educational agencies, and States accountable for improving the academic achievement of all students, and identifying and turning around low-performing schools that have failed to provide a high-quality education to their students, while providing alternatives to students in such schools to enable the students to receive a high-quality education;

(5) distributing and targeting resources sufficiently to make a difference to local educational agencies and schools where needs are greatest;

(6) improving and strengthening accountability, teaching, and learning by using State assessment systems designed to ensure that students are meeting challenging State academic achievement and content standards and increasing achievement overall, but especially for the disadvantaged;

(7) providing greater decisionmaking authority and flexibility to schools and teachers in exchange for greater responsibility for student performance;

(8) providing children an enriched and accelerated educational program, including the use of schoolwide programs or additional services that increase the amount and quality of instructional time;

(9) promoting schoolwide reform and ensuring the access of children to effective, scientifically based instructional strategies and challenging academic content;

(10) significantly elevating the quality of instruction by providing staff in participating schools with substantial opportunities for professional development;

(11) coordinating services under all parts of this title with each other, with other educational services, and, to the extent feasible, with other agencies providing services to youth, children, and families; and

(12) affording parents substantial and meaningful opportunities to participate in the education of their children.

No Child Left Behind requires that all children be assessed. In order to show adequate yearly progress, schools must test at least 95 percent of the various subgroups of children, including students with disabilities. States must provide reasonable accommodations for students with disabilities.

CHAPTER 9:
TRANSITIONING YOUR CHILD FROM SCHOOL TO THE WORKPLACE

HELPING YOUR CHILD MAKE THE TRANSITION

While in school, if your child had a physical or emotional problem, the school would arrange for an evaluation to determine whether special education and related services were necessary to help your child succeed in school. Under The Individuals With Disabilities Education Act (IDEA), it was the school's responsibility to identify and meet your child's needs, and your child was entitled to these services.

The IDEA is discussed more fully in Chapter 8 of this almanac.

Once your child has graduated from high school, he or she is no longer protected under the IDEA. Many parents worry that their child will be unable to make a successful transition from school to entering the workforce without the support he or she was getting in school. However, there are many organizations who are ready and willing to help your child succeed in this transition.

A transitioning resource directory is set forth at Appendix 14.

Even though your child is no longer covered under the IDEA, he or she is still eligible to receive accommodations provided he or she is deemed a qualified individual with a disability under the law. The difference now is that your child has to take on much of the responsibility of identifying his or her needs, describing the impact of his or her disability, and explaining the type of accommodation needed to succeed in the workforce. Your child becomes his or her own best advocate.

As a parent, you also play an important role in this transitioning stage. Find out what resources and supports are available in your community for adults with disabilities. Don't wait until your child graduates to start educating yourself as to what's available. Your child's IEP should contain a transition plan outlining the goals and steps that must be taken to make the transition from school to employment easier.

Your child's transition plan should include testing and activities that help identify your child's interests, strengths and abilities. The plan should also include activities that teach your child the skills necessary to find and maintain employment. Early work experiences, paid or unpaid, can positively impact future employment abilities and opportunities.

You can help your child prepare for his or her future by helping them explore their interests, strengths, and abilities, and discussing with them how they might relate to possible career choices. Find out if there is a particular school subject that interests your child, such as math or art. What subjects does he or she do well in versus those in which he or she struggles? Does your child enjoy being outdoors? Does your child like working with tools and fixing things? Take note of your child's hobbies, likes and dislikes. These are some informal ways that may indicate your child's interests, strengths and abilities.

There are also tests that your child can take that identify interests. Gathering this information can guide you and your child to possible career choices. In addition, school guidance counselors and special education teachers can provide you with additional information on career planning.

You should expect your child to achieve to the best of his or her abilities, however limited, and insist that everyone who plays an important role in his or her life have the same expectations. As your child gets older, you should help him or her learn about important disability-related laws, investigate resources together, encourage your child to meet with school guidance counselors and career planning representatives, and most important, ensure that he has many age-appropriate opportunities throughout his or her life to develop the skills needed to transition into adulthood.

WORK-BASED LEARNING ACTIVITIES

You should also encourage your child to take advantage of work-based learning activities which will help your child obtain first-hand experience and knowledge about various careers pathways. Your child will also benefit by learning responsibility, timeliness, proper dress, and how to get along with co-workers and supervisors.

Children with disabilities have the same opportunities for work-based learning as any child, however, your child may need to discuss the availability of needed accommodations with the employer. Although your child is not required to tell an employer about their disability, there are advantages to disclosing this information. For example, your child is entitled to certain rights under the Americans with Disabilities Act (ADA), as discussed below. If your child discloses his or her disability to the employer, this will ensure that your child will receive the accommodations and supports needed to succeed.

Following are some of the various types of work-based learning experiences in which your child can participate:

Information Interviews

An information interview is a meeting with people working in a particular field your child may be interested in so he or she can ask questions about jobs in the field.

Job Shadowing

Job shadowing involves spending time observing a worker carrying out his or her daily activities in a particular job or industry.

Internships

An internship provides a short-term on-the-job work experience in a particular field under the supervision of the employer. An internship may be paid or unpaid. Volunteer work provides essentially the same work-based learning experience as an internship.

Apprenticeship

An apprenticeship provides the opportunity to attend training classes and learn skills from workers in a particular field over a long period of time, e.g. 2-5 years. Apprenticeships are generally paid positions. Therefore, if your child receives Supplemental Security Income (SSI) due to his or her disabilities, you need to consider how it will impact your child's benefits, as set forth in Chapter 7 of this almanac.

EMPLOYMENT DISCRIMINATION

It is important for children with disabilities and their families to understand disability legislation and the rights the child is entitled to under the law once they are no longer in the school setting. For example, the Americans with Disabilities Act (ADA) prohibits, in part, discrimination on the basis of disability in employment. The ADA's employment provisions include the following:

1. The ADA requires equal opportunity in selection, testing and hiring of qualified applicants with disabilities.

2. The ADA prohibits discrimination against workers with disabilities.

3. The ADA employment provisions apply to private employers, State and local governments, employment agencies, labor organizations, and joint labor-management committees.

4. The ADA requires equal treatment in promotion and benefits.

5. The ADA requires reasonable accommodation for applicants and workers with disabilities when such accommodations would not impose "undue hardship."

6. Employers may not make pre-employment inquiries about an applicant's disability or conduct pre-employment medical exams. They may ask if applicants can perform specific job functions and may condition a job offer on results of a medical exam, but only if the exam is required for all entering employees in similar jobs.

THE NATIONAL COLLABORATIVE ON WORKFORCE AND DISABILITY

The National Collaborative on Workforce and Disability (NCWD/Youth) is an important source for information about employment and youth with disabilities. The NCWD/Youth assists state and local workforce development systems to better serve youth with disabilities.

NCWD/Youth, created in late 2001, is composed of partners with expertise in disability, education, employment, and workforce development issues, and funded by a grant from the U.S. Department of Labor's Office of Disability Employment Policy.

NCWD/Youth research has identified the following operating principles as being vital in effective transition programs for all youth:

1. Access to high quality standards-based education regardless of the setting;

2. Information about career options;

3. Exposure to the world of work;

4. Opportunities to develop social, civic, and leadership skills;

5. Strong connections to caring adults;

6. Access to safe places to interact with their peers, and

7. Support services to allow them to become independent adults.

Based upon these operating principles, NCWD/Youth recognizes the following four features of effective programs and services:

Preparatory Experiences

Preparatory Experiences are those core activities that help youth become prepared for a successful future in careers or postsecondary education institutions. They include the career interest and vocational assessments, information about careers, income potential, and work-readiness skills.

Work-Based Learning

As discussed above, work-based learning occurs in supervised programs sponsored by an education or training organization and links knowledge gained at the worksite with a planned program of study. Experiences range in intensity, structure and scope and include activities as diverse as site visits, job shadowing, paid and unpaid internships, structured on-the-job training, and the more formal work status as apprentice or employee.

Youth Development & Youth Leadership

Youth Development & Youth Leadership are processes that prepare young people to meet the challenges of adolescence and adulthood through a coordinated, progressive series of activities and experiences. These include providing structured relationships with adults and exposing every youth to personal leadership skills such as self-advocacy and self-determination.

Connecting Activities

Connecting Activities provide necessary support services for youth and enrich program content. They include academic tutoring, adult and peer mentoring, and helping youth explore self-sufficiency issues like assistive technology, transportation, benefits planning, and health maintenance.

ONE-STOPS

"One-Stops" are clearinghouses of job information and resources related to employment which are mandated by the Workforce Investment Act (WIA) to promote "universal access"—i.e., they strive to meet everyone's unique user needs. A One-Stop can help you find out about and link to a variety of services, and is a valuable resource to those individuals transitioning to the workforce.

One-Stop staff can help find information about careers in a child's local community and the skills they require; help them gain the skills to conduct job searches, write resumes, and prepare for interviews; access information and opportunities for work-based experience through internships, summer work programs, apprenticeships and mentoring; and help them to identify community resources that can help them to plan and meet their transition goals.

Most One-Stop Centers will have an intake form that may have a question on it about the presence of a disability, however, disclosing one's disability is totally your child's decision. Nevertheless, if your child will need assistance or some type of accommodation to access services and use them to their benefit, it is advisable to disclose their disability.

A database of One-Stop Centers, searchable by state, can be found at the following Department of Labor website: http://www.doleta.gov/usworkforce/onestop/ which you can search by state.

THE TICKET TO WORK PROGRAM

On December 17, 1999, the Ticket to Work program was enacted as part of the "Ticket to Work and Work Incentives Improvement Act of 1999 (TWWIIA)" under the Social Security Administration. The Ticket to Work program provides support for disabled persons over the age of 18 who receive Supplemental Security Income (SSI) or Social Security Disability Income (SSDI) as they move into employment.

As of September 2004, the Ticket to Work program was available in all 50 States, the District of Columbia, as well as all the U.S. territories. You can obtain further information about the Ticket to Work program by calling the Ticket to Work Help Line toll free at 1-866-YOUR-TICKET (1-866-968- 7842) or 1-866-833-2967 (TTY).

A table setting forth the number of tickets issued as of May, 2005, by state, is set forth at Appendix 15.

Title I

Under Title I of the TWWIIA, employment support is offered to SSI and SSDI recipients who will receive a "ticket" from the SSA to one of several employment networks and/or Vocational Rehabilitation agencies. The ticket will allow the recipient to obtain a variety of services including job search, job training, job coaching, etc.

The Ticket is a paper document that has some personal information about the person receiving it and some general information about the Ticket Program. You take your Ticket to an Employment Network or to the State Vocational Rehabilitation Agency. The Employment Networks are private organizations or public agencies, that have agreed to work with Social Security to provide services under this program.

You can contact any Employment Network in your area to see if it is the right one for you. Both you and the Employment Network have to agree to work together to attain your employment goals. You are free to talk with as many Employment Networks as you choose without having to give one your Ticket. You can also stop working with one Employment

Network and begin working with another one, or with the State Vocational Rehabilitation Agency.

Title II

Under Title II of the TWWIIA, two new optional Medicaid eligibility categories were created. The first is called the "Basic Coverage Group". Under this option, states can offer Medicaid to working adults (ages 16-65) with disabilities who would qualify for Medicaid, except for their income and resources, including both persons who never received SSI as well as those leaving SSI for work. States can set their own income limits or other related standards.

The second category is called the "Medical Improvement Group". Under this option, states may elect to continue to offer Medicaid to working persons with disabilities whose disability has improved to the point where they are no longer SSI eligible. States that opt for the second coverage group must also cover the first group. States may also charge premiums, or fees on a sliding scale basis under either of these eligibility groups.

As part of the Act, two new grant programs were established to assist states in implementing these provisions. The Medicaid Infrastructure Grant Program provides grants to states to help them design and operate health care delivery systems that support the employment of persons with disabilities. One criterion states must meet to be eligible for these grants is that they offer personal assistance to working individuals with disabilities.

A second grant program, the Medicaid Demonstration to Increase Independence and Employment grant offers states an opportunity to create demonstration programs for assisting persons who are at-risk for developing blindness or disability with early access to Medicaid and employment services.

CHAPTER 10: PLANNING YOUR ESTATE WHEN YOU HAVE A CHALLENGED CHILD

PLANNING AHEAD

If you have a child who will never be able to live independently without assistance, it is important to plan for the care of your child upon your death. In order to properly do so, you must have a thorough understanding of your child's needs; and you must understand the alternative estate planning methods that are available to protect disabled children both personally and financially.

Estate planning means to make plans for the disposition of your property upon your death to your beneficiaries, primarily your children and your spouse, if married. Usually, one leaves their property to their beneficiaries without trying to limit what the beneficiaries can do with the property. However, this plan will not work for many children with disabilities. Allowing a disabled child to inherit your property without any control or limitation is risky. For example:

1. He or she may not be able to handle the funds properly;

2. If the disabled child who inherits the property is in a state institution, the state will then bill the disabled child for the cost of their care;

3. If the disabled child is not in an institution, he or she may lose welfare or supplemental social security benefits, which are necessary for the child to be able to continue to live on his or her own or in a group setting.

The topic of estate planning is discussed more thoroughly in this author's legal almanac entitled "Estate Planning," published by Oceana Publishing Company.

YOUR WILL

One of the most important estate planning documents is your will. Your will names the beneficiaries of your estate, names a personal representative to administer your will, and makes provisions for your minor or incapacitated children. It is particularly important in the case of a disabled child that your will have provisions for personal protection of your child.

Depending on your wishes, and your child's limitations, there are several ways to protect your child in your will. As discussed below, your will can name a certain individual to step in and take your place upon your death in order to make sure your wishes for your child's care, support, medical needs, housing, education, social and spiritual needs are followed.

Name an Advisor

You can name an "advisor" for your child, who will offer guidance and suggestions to a child who is able to make decisions about his or her personal or financial affairs independently. This is the least restrictive form of personal protection for your child.

Name an Advocate

If you believe your child will need more protection, you can name an "advocate" for your child. An advocate will assume greater responsibility for your child than an advisor. For example, in addition to the responsibilities of an advisor, the advocate will speak on behalf of your child; monitor services; and may represent the person's interests. However, neither an advisor nor an advocate can legally impose his or her wishes on the person represented.

Name a Guardian

The most restrictive form of personal protection for your child is a "guardianship." A guardian is sometimes appointed by the court. The guardian can make decisions if your child is incapacitated to the extent that he or she is unable to effectively make decisions. For example, the guardian may decide where your child will live, and can also consent to your child's medical treatment. The term "incapacitated" means one whose ability to receive and evaluate information effectively or make decisions is impaired to an extent that the person cannot meet his or her physical, health or safety needs.

Parents are the natural guardians of their child only until the child reaches age 18, whether the child is incapacitated or not. If your child is incapacitated after he or she reaches age 18, you may wish to seek court appointment as your child's legal guardian with the further provision that, in the event of the death of one parent, the surviving parent will remain as sole guardian.

Parents who think that their child will need a guardianship upon their deaths should nominate a guardian in their wills. The court must ultimately make the choice of guardian, and will define the scope of the guardianship, such as whether the guardian will have full powers or be limited to making only certain types of decisions, such as medical treatment.

Court-Appointed Conservator

Your will should consider your disabled child's financial security. As set forth above, a direct inheritance of money or property to a disabled child may make the child ineligible for certain federal and state benefits. In addition, if the child is institutionalized, a direct inheritance of money or property may be claimed by the state as reimbursement for institutional care furnished to the child.

If you still want to leave the inheritance to your child, but fear that your child is incapable of managing the money or property, you may appoint a "conservator" for your child in your will. A conservator is a person appointed by the court to handle the property of a minor or incapacitated person.

Because of the cost involved, a convservatorship may be advisable only under certain circumstances. For example, if the child's finances consist only of government support, such as SSI, Social Security, or veterans' benefits, the federal agency can set up a Representative Payee, naming someone to handle those funds on the child's behalf at no cost to the child and without court involvement.

TRUSTS

Another estate planning tool that may be useful in insuring financial security for your child is a trust. A trust names a trustee who manages property for your child and pays the child's expenses or gives him or her money according to guidelines specified in your trust.

Support Trust

You may form a "support trust" while you are still alive. The advantage of this type of trust is that there will be no interruption in the financial support of the disabled child upon your death while your estate is being probated. However, this type of trust can also be set up in your will, which means it will only go into effect upon your death. The support trust should be flexible in case your child's needs change in the future, and the trustee should be given wide discretion to use the trust income and assets in various ways to meet your child's needs.

Special Needs Trust

Another type of trust is the "special needs trust," also referred to as a "supplemental needs trust." This type of trust is used when a child is receiving or may receive need-based governmental benefits, such as Supplemental Security Income (SSI) or Medicaid.

To be eligible for SSI and Medicaid, your child must have minimal income and assets. Therefore, you potentially jeopardize your child's eligibility every time you save for his or her future care. However, because the funds in a special needs trust are managed by a trustee and legally do not belong to your child, they are not considered "countable" for SSI and Medicaid eligibility purposes.

Thus, it is crucial that the language of the trust document conform with current laws and regulations. If the trust is not drafted properly, the governmental benefit could be lost, and the trust money dissipated before your child can reapply for government benefits.

To avoid having the state claim that the trust proceeds must be used to support your child, the trust document must state that the principal and income are to be used only to provide supplemental care, maintenance, and support that is not provided for by the government benefits, such as clothes, personal items, etc.

Once you have created the trust, you can fund it with any asset you choose, such as cash, stocks, etc. Term or cash value life insurance can also be used to fund a special needs trust. The trust would own the life insurance policy or would be a named beneficiary of the policy upon your death.

APPENDIX 1:
ADVOCACY GROUPS FOR PARENTS OF DISABLED CHILDREN

ORGANIZATION	ADDRESS	TELEPHONE	FAX	E-MAIL	WEBSITE
Family Voices	3411 Candelana NE, Suite M, Albuquerque, NM 87107	505-872-4774	505-872-4780	kidshealth@familyvoices.org	www.familyvoices.org
Minnesota Early Learning Design (MELD)	123 N. Third St., Suite 507, Minneapolis, MN 55401	612-332-7563	612-332-7563	info@meld.org	www.meld.org
Mothers From Hell 2	P.O. Box 19, German Valley, IL 61039	815-362-5303	303-374-3151	beth@mothersfromhell2.org	www.mothersfromhell2.org

ADVOCACY GROUPS FOR PARENTS OF DISABLED CHILDREN

ORGANIZATION	ADDRESS	TELEPHONE	FAX	E-MAIL	WEBSITE
National Challenged Homeschoolers (NATHHAN)	P.O. Box 39, Porthill, ID 83853	208-267-6246	none listed	nathanews@aol.com	www.nathhan.com
Parent Network for the Post-Institutionalized Child (PNPIC)	P.O. Box 613, Meadow Lands, PA 15347	724-222-1766	none listed	none listed	PNPIC.org
Parents Helping Parents (PHP)	3041 Olcott St., Santa Clara, CA 95054-3222	408-727-5775	408-748-8339	info@php.com	www.php.com
Parents Are Vital in Education (PAVE)	6316 S. 12Th, Tacoma, WA 98465	253-565-2266	253-566-8052	wapave9@washingtonpave.org	www.washingtonpave.org
Birth Defect Research for Children	930 Woodcock Rd., Suite 225, Orlando, FL 32803	407-895-0802	407-895-0824	abdc@birthdefects.org	www.birthdefects.org
Sibling Support Project of the Arc of the United States	6512 23rd Ave. NW, #213, Seattle, WA 98117	206-297-6368	509-752-6789	none listed	www.thearc.org/siblingsupport/
Washington State Fathers Network	16120 N.E. Eighth. St., Bellevue, WA 98008	425-747-4004	none listed	cmorris@fathersnetwork.org	www.fathersnetwork.org

ADVOCACY GROUPS FOR PARENTS OF DISABLED CHILDREN

ORGANIZATION	ADDRESS	TELEPHONE	FAX	E-MAIL	WEBSITE
Our-Kids	none listed	none listed	none listed	none listed	www.ourkids.org
Siblings for Significant Change	350 Fifth Ave., Room 627, New York, NY 10118	212-643-2663	212-643-1244	none listed	www.meld.org
MUMS National Parent-to-Parent Network	150 Custer Court, Green Bay, WI 54301-1234	920-336-5333	920-339-0995	mums@netnet.net	www.netnet.net/mums
National Information Center for Children and Youth with Disabilities (NICHCY)	P.O. Box 1492, Washington, DC 20013	202-884-8200	none listed	nichcy@aed.org	www.nichcy.org
ERIC Clearinghouse on Disabilities and Gifted Education (ERIC EC)	1920 Association Drive, Reston, VA 20191-1589	800-328-0272	none listed	ericec@cec.sped.org	ericec.org
Technical Assistance for Parent Centers—the Alliance	PACER Center, 4826 Chicago Avenue South, Minneapolis, MN 55417-1098	612-827-2966	none listed	alliance@taalliance.org	www.taalliance.org
The Council for Exceptional Children	1920 Association Drive, Reston, VA 20191-1589	703-264-9456	none listed	ideapractices@cec.sped.org	www.ideapractices.org

How to Protect Your Challenged Child

ADVOCACY GROUPS FOR PARENTS OF DISABLED CHILDREN

ORGANIZATION	ADDRESS	TELEPHONE	FAX	E-MAIL	WEBSITE
Families and Advocates Partnerships for Education (FAPE)	4826 Chicago Avenue South, Minneapolis, MN 55417-1098	612-827-2966	none listed	fape@pacer.org	www.fape.org
The Policy Maker Partnership (PMP), National Association of State Directors of Special Education	1800 Diagonal Road, Suite 320, Alexandria, VA 22314	703-519-3800	none listed	nasdse@nasdse.org	www.nasdse.org
Northeast Regional Resource Center (NERRC)	20 Winter Sport Lane, Williston, VT 05495	802-951-8226	none listed	nerrc@aol.com	www.wested.org/nerrc/
Mid-South Regional Resource Center (MSRRC)	126 Mineral Industries Building, Lexington, KY 40506-0051	859-257-4921	none listed	msrrc@ihdi.uky.edu	www.ihdi.uky.edu/msrrc
Southeast Regional Resource Center (SERRC)	P.O. Box 244023, Montgomery, AL 36124	334-244-3100	none listed	ebeale@mail.aum.edu	edla.aum.edu/serrc/serrc.html
Great Lakes Area Regional Resource Center (GLARRC)	700 Ackerman Road, Suite 440 Columbus, OH 43202	614-447-0844	none listed	daniels.121@osu.edu	www.csnp.ohio-state.edu/glarrc.htm

ADVOCACY GROUPS FOR PARENTS OF DISABLED CHILDREN

ORGANIZATION	ADDRESS	TELEPHONE	FAX	E-MAIL	WEBSITE
Mountain Plains Regional Resource Center (MPRRC)	1780 North Research Parkway, Suite 112, Logan, UT 84341	435-752-0238	none listed	cope@cc.usu.edu	www.usu.edu/mprrc
Western Regional Resource Center (WRRC)	1268 University of Oregon, Eugene, OR 97403-1268	541-346-5641	none listed	wrrc@oregon.uoregon.edu	interact.uoregon.edu/wrrc/wrrc.html
Pacer Center	8161 Normandale Blvd, Minneapolis, MN 55437-1044	952-838-9000	952-838-0199	alliance@taalliance.org	www.taalliance.org
Statewide Parent Advocacy Network (SPAN)	35 Halsey Street, 4th Floor, Newark, NJ 07102	973-642-8100	973-642-8080	span@spannj.org	www.spannj.org
Exceptional Children's Assistance Center (ECAC)	907 Barra Row, Suite 102/103, Davidson, NC 28036	704-892-1321	704-892-5028	ecacta@ecacmail.org	www.ecac-parentcenter.org
Family Network on Disabilities of Florida, Inc.	2735 Whitney Road, Clearwater, FL 33760-1610	727-525-1130	727-523-8687	fnd@fndfl.org	www.fndfl.org

How to Protect Your Challenged Child

ADVOCACY GROUPS FOR PARENTS OF DISABLED CHILDREN

ORGANIZATION	ADDRESS	TELEPHONE	FAX	E-MAIL	WEBSITE
Ohio Coalition for the Education of Children with Disabilities (OCECD)	Bank One Building, 165 West Center Street, Suite 302, Marion, OH 43302-3741	740-382-5452	740-383-6421	ocecd@gte.net	www.ocecd.org
PEAK Parent Center, Inc.	611 North Weber, Suite 200, Colorado Springs, CO 80903	719-531-9400	719-531-9452	info@peakparent.org	www.peakparent.org
Matrix Parent Network and Resource Center	94 Galli Drive, Suite C, Novato, CA 94949	415-884-3535	415-884-3555	none listed	www.matrixparents.org
Native American Families Together Parent Center	129 West Third, Moscow, ID 83843	208-885-3500	208-885-3628	NAFT@moscow.com	www.nativefamilynetwork.com
PAVE/STOMP	6316 South 12th St., Suite B, Tacoma, WA 98465-1900	253-565-2266	253-566-8052	stomp@washingtonpave.com	www.stompproject.org

APPENDIX 2:
NATIONAL DISABILITY ORGANIZATIONS

ORGANIZATION	ADDRESS	TELEPHONE	EMAIL	WEBSITE
Alexander Graham Bell Association for the Deaf and Hard of Hearing	3417 Volta Place N.W., Washington, DC 20007	(202) 337-5220	parents@agbell.org	www.agbell.org
Alliance for Technology Access	1304 Southpoint Blvd., Suite 240, Petaluma, CA 94954	(707) 778-3011	atainfo@ataccess.org	www.ataccess.org
American Association of Kidney Patients (AAKP)	3505 Frontage Road, Suite 315, Tampa, FL 33607	(800) 749-2257	info@aakp.org	www.aakp.org
American Association of Suicidology	5221 Wisconsin Avenue N.W., Washington, DC 20015	(202) 237-2280	info@suicidology.org	www.suicidology.org
American Brain Tumor Association	2720 River Road, Des Moines, IA 60018	(847) 827-9910	info@abta.org	www.abta.org

NATIONAL DISABILITY ORGANIZATIONS

ORGANIZATION	ADDRESS	TELEPHONE	EMAIL	WEBSITE
American Council of the Blind	1155 15th Street N.W., Suite 1004, Washington, DC 20005	(202) 467-5081	info@acb.org	www.acb.org
American Diabetes Association	1701 N. Beauregard Street, Alexandria, VA 22311	(703) 549-1500	AskADA@diabetes.org	www.diabetes.org
American Foundation for the Blind (AFB)	11 Penn Plaza, Suite 300, New York, NY 10001	(212) 502-7662	afbinfo@afb.net	www.afb.org
American Heart Association-National Center	7272 Greenville Avenue, Dallas, TX 75231	(214) 373-6300	inquire@amhrt.org	www.americanheart.org
American Liver Foundation	75 Maiden Lane, Suite 603, New York, NY 10038	(212) 668-1000	info@liverfoundation.org	www.liverfoundation.org
American Lung Association	61 Broadway, 6th Floor, New York, NY 10006	(212) 315-8700	E-mail via website	www.lungusa.org
American Occupational Therapy Association (AOTA)	4720 Montgomery Lane, P.O. Box 31220, Bethesda, MD 20824-1220	(301) 652-2682	none listed	www.aota.org
American Physical Therapy Association (APTA)	1111 North Fairfax Street, Alexandria, VA 22314	(703) 684-2782	practice@apta.org	www.apta.org
American Society for Deaf Children	P.O. Box 3355, Gettysburg, PA 17325	(800) 942-2732	asdc@deafchildren.org	www.deafchildren.org
American Speech-Language-Hearing Association (ASHA)	10801 Rockville Pike, Rockville, MD 20852	(301) 897-5700	actioncenter@asha.org	www.asha.org

NATIONAL DISABILITY ORGANIZATIONS

ORGANIZATION	ADDRESS	TELEPHONE	EMAIL	WEBSITE
American Syringomyelia Alliance Project	P.O. Box 1586, Longview, TX 75606-1586	(903) 236-7079	info@asap.org	www.asap.org
American Therapeutic Recreation Association	1414 Prince Street, Suite 204, Alexandria, VA 22314	(703) 683-9420	atra@atra-tr.org	www.atra-tr.org
Angelman Syndrome Foundation	3015 E. New York Street, Suite A2265, Aurora, IL 60504	(630) 978-4245	info@angelman.org	www.angelman.org
Anxiety Disorders Association of America	8730 Georgia Avenue, Suite 600, Silver Spring, MD 20910	(240) 485-1001	AnxDis@adaa.org	www.adaa.org
Aplastic Anemia &MDS International Foundation, Inc.	P. O. Box 613, Annapolis, MD 21404-0613	(410) 867-0242	help@aamds.org	www.aamds.org
The Arc (formerly the Association for Retarded Citizens of the U.S.)	1010 Wayne Avenue, Suite 650, Silver Spring, MD 20910	(301) 565-3842	Info@thearc.org	www.thearc.org
ARCH National Respite Network & Resource Center	800 Eastowne Drive, Suite 105, Chapel Hill, NC 27514,	(919) 490-5577	none listed	www.archrespite.org
Arthritis Foundation	P.O. Box 7669, Atlanta, GA 30357	(404) 872-7100	help@arthritis.org	www.arthritis.org
Asthma and Allergy Foundation of America	1233 20th Street, N.W. Suite 402, Washington, DC 20036	(202) 466-7643	info@aafa.org	www.aafa.org

How to Protect Your Challenged Child

NATIONAL DISABILITY ORGANIZATIONS

ORGANIZATION	ADDRESS	TELEPHONE	EMAIL	WEBSITE
Autism Society of America	7910 Woodmont Avenue, Suite 300, Bethesda, MD 20814-3015	(301) 657-0881	info@autism-society.org	www.autism-society.org
Beach Center on Disability	1200 Sunnyside Avenue, Lawrence, KS 66045-7534	(785) 864-7600	beachcenter@ku.edu	www.beachcenter.org
Best Buddies International, Inc.	100 S.E. Second Street, Suite 1990, Miami, FL 33131	(305) 374-2233	info@bestbuddies.org	www.bestbuddies.org
Blind Childrens Center	4120 Marathon Street, Los Angeles, CA 90029-0159	(323) 664-2153	info@blindchildrenscenter.org	www.blindchildrenscenter.org
Brain Injury Association of America	8201 Greensboro Dr., Suite 611, McLean, VA 22102	(703) 761-0750	FamilyHelpline@biausa.org	www.biausa.org
CADRE (Consortium for Appropriate Dispute Resolution in Special Education)	Direction Service, Inc., P.O. Box 51360, Eugene, OR 97405-0906	(541) 686-5060	cadre@directionservice.org	www.directionservice.org/cadre
Center for Effective Collaboration and Practice (CECP), (Improving Services for Children and Youth with Emotional and Behavioral Problems)	1000 Thomas Jefferson St., N.W., Suite 400, Washington, DC 20007	(202) 944-5300	center@air.org	cecp.air.org
Center for Evidence Based Practice: Young Children with Challenging Behavior	13301 Bruce B. Downs Blvd., Tampa, FL 33612-3807	(813) 974-6111	dunlap@fmhi.usf.edu	challengingbehavior.fmhi.usf.edu

NATIONAL DISABILITY ORGANIZATIONS

ORGANIZATION	ADDRESS	TELEPHONE	EMAIL	WEBSITE
Center for Universal Design	Campus Box 8613, Raleigh, NC 27695-8613	(919) 515-3082	cud@ncsu.edu	www.design.ncsu.edu/cud
Child and Adolescent Bipolar Foundation	1000 Skokie Blvd., Suite 425, Wilmette, IL 60091	(847) 256-8525	cabf@bpkids.org	www.bpkids.org
Childhood Apraxia of Speech Association of North America (CASANA)	123 Eisele Road, Cheswick, PA 15024	(412) 767-6589	helpdesk@apraxia-kids.org	www.apraxia-kids.org
Children and Adults with Attention-Deficit/Hyperactivity Disorder (CHADD)	8181 Professional Place, Suite 150, Landover, MD 20785	(301) 306-7070	none listed	www.chadd.org
Children's Craniofacial Association	13140 Coit Road, Suite 307, Dallas, TX 75240	(214) 570-9099	contact CCA@ccakids.com	www.ccakids.com
Children's Tumor Foundation	95 Pine Street, 16th Floor, New York, NY 10005	(212) 344-6633	info@ctf.org	www.ctf.org
Chronic Fatigue and Immune Dysfunction Syndrome Association (CFIDS)	P.O. Box 220398, Charlotte, NC 28222-0398	(704) 365-2343	cfids@cfids.org	www.cfids.org
Closing the Gap Inc.	P.O. Box 68, 526 Main Street, Henderson, MN 56044	(507) 248-3294	None listed	www.closingthegap.com

NATIONAL DISABILITY ORGANIZATIONS

ORGANIZATION	ADDRESS	TELEPHONE	EMAIL	WEBSITE
Council for Exceptional Children (CEC)	1110 N. Glebe Road, Suite 300, Arlington, VA 22201-5704	(703) 620-3660	service@cec.sped.org	www.cec.sped.org
Craniofacial Foundation of America	975 East Third Street, Box 269, Chattanooga, TN 37403	(423) 778-9192	farmertm@erlanger.org	www.erlanger.org/craniofacial/found1.html,
Crohn's &Colitis Foundation of America	386 Park Avenue South, 17th Foor, New York, NY 10016	(212) 685-3440	info@ccfa.org	www.ccfa.org
Cystic Fibrosis Foundation	6931 Arlington Road, Bethesda, MD 20814	(301) 951-4422	info@cff.org	www.cff.org
Depression and Bipolar Support Alliance	730 N. Franklin Street, Suite 501, Chicago, IL 60610,	(312) 642-0049	questions@dbsalliance.org	www.dbsalliance.org
Disability Statistics Rehabilitation Research and Training Center	3333 California Street, Room 340, San Francisco, CA 94118	(415) 502-5210	distats@itsa.ucsf.edu	www.dsc.ucsf.edu
Disabled Sports USA	451 Hungerford Drive, Suite 100, Rockville, MD 20850	(301) 217-0960	Information@dsusa.org	www.dsusa.org
Easter Seals	230 West Monroe Street, Suite 1800, Chicago, IL 60606	312) 726-6200	info@easter-seals.org	www.easter-seals.org

NATIONAL DISABILITY ORGANIZATIONS

ORGANIZATION	ADDRESS	TELEPHONE	EMAIL	WEBSITE
Epilepsy Foundation-National Office	4351 Garden City Drive, 5th Floor, Landover, MD 20785-4941,	(301) 459-3700	E-mail via website.	www.epilepsyfoundation.org
FACES: The National Craniofacial Association	P.O. Box 11082, Chattanooga, TN 37401,	(423) 266-1632	faces@faces-cranio.org	www.faces-cranio.org
Family Center for Technology and Disabilities	1825 Connecticut Avenue, NW, 7th Floor, Washington, DC 20009-5721	(202) 884-8068	fctd@aed.org	www.fctd.info
Family Empowerment Network: Support for Families Affected by FAS/E	772 S. Mills Street, Madison, WI 53715	(608) 262-6590	fen@fammed.wisc.edu	www.fammed.wisc.edu/fen
Family Resource Center on Disabilities	20 East Jackson Boulevard, Room 300, Chicago, IL 60604	(312) 939-3513	none listed	www.frcd.org
Family Village	1500 Highland Avenue, Madison, WI 53705-2280	(608) 263-5776	familyvillage@waisman.wisc.edu	www.familyvillage.wisc.edu
Family Voices	2340 Alamo SE, Suite 102, Albuquerque, NM 87106	(505) 872-4774	kidshealth@familyvoices.org	www.familyvoices.org
Federation of Families for Children's Mental Health	1101 King Street, Suite 420, Alexandria, VA 22314	(703) 684-7710	ffcmh@ffcmh.com	www.ffcmh.org
First Signs Inc.	P.O. Box 358, Merrimac, MA 01860	(978) 346-4380	info@firstsigns.org	www.firstsigns.org

How to Protect Your Challenged Child

NATIONAL DISABILITY ORGANIZATIONS

ORGANIZATION	ADDRESS	TELEPHONE	EMAIL	WEBSITE
Forward Face	317 East 34th Street, Suite 901A, New York, NY 10016	(212) 684-5860	info@forwardface.org	www.forwardface.org
Foundation for Ichthyosis and Related Skin Types	1601 Valley Forge Road, Lansdale, PA 19446	(215) 631-1411	info@scalyskin.org	www.scalyskin.org
Genetic Alliance	4301 Connecticut N.W., Suite 404, Washington,. DC 20008	(202) 966-5557	info@geneticalliance.org	www.geneticalliance.org
Head Start Bureau	P.O. Box 1182, Washington, DC 20013	none listed	www.acf.dhhs.gov/programs/hsb	
Human Growth Foundation	997 Glen Cove Avenue, Suite 5, Glen Head, NY 11545	(800) 451-6434	hgf1@hgfound.org	www.hgfound.org
Huntington's Disease Society of America	158 West 29th Street, 7th Floor, New York, NY 10001-5300	(212) 242-1968	hdsainfo@hdsa.org	www.hdsa.org
Hydrocephalus Association	870 Market Street, #705, San Francisco, CA 94102	(415) 732-7040	info@hydroassoc.org	www.hydroassoc.org
IBM Accessability Center	11400 Burnet Road, Austin, TX 78758	(800) 426-4832	E-mail via website.	www-3.ibm.com/able/index.html
Immune Deficiency Foundation	40 W. Chesapeake Avenue, Suite 308, Towson, MD 21204	(800) 296-4433	idf@primaryimmune.org	www.primaryimmune.org

NATIONAL DISABILITY ORGANIZATIONS

ORGANIZATION	ADDRESS	TELEPHONE	EMAIL	WEBSITE
Independent Living Research Utilization Project	The Institute for Rehabilitation and Research, 2323 South Sheppard, Suite 1000, Houston, TX 77019	(713) 520-0232	ilru@ilru.org	www.ilru.org
International Dyslexia Association	Chester Building, #382, 8600 LaSalle Road, Baltimore, MD 21286-2044	(410) 296-0232	info@interdys.org	www.interdys.org
International Resource Center for Down Syndrome	1621 Euclid Avenue, Suite 802, Cleveland, OH 44115	(216) 621-5858	none listed	none listed
International Rett Syndrome Association	9121 Piscataway Rd., Clinton, MD 20735-2561	(301) 856-3334	irsa@rettsyndrome.org	www.rettsyndrome.org
Job Accommodation Network (JAN)	P.O. Box 6080, Morgantown, WV 26506-6080	(800) 526-7234	jan@jan.wvu.edu	www.jan.wvu.edu
Kristin Brooks Hope Center	2001 N. Beauregard St., 12th floor, Alexandria, VA 22311	(703) 837-3364	info@hopeline.com	www.livewithdepression.org
Learning Disabilities Association of America (LDA)	4156 Library Road, Pittsburgh, PA 15234	(412) 341-1515	info@ldaamerica.org	www.ldaamerica.org
Let's Face It USA	P.O. Box 29972, Bellingham, WA 98228-1972	(360) 676-7325	letsfaceit@faceit.org	www.faceit.org
Leukemia & Lymphoma Society	1311 Mamaroneck Ave., White Plains, NY 10605	(914) 949-5213	infocenter@leukemia-lymphoma.org	www.leukemia-lymphoma.org

NATIONAL DISABILITY ORGANIZATIONS

ORGANIZATION	ADDRESS	TELEPHONE	EMAIL	WEBSITE
Little People of America	5289 NE Elam Young Parkway, Suite F-100, Hillsboro, OR 97124	(888) 572-2001	info@lpaonline.org	www.lpaonline.org
Lupus Foundation of America	2000 L Street NW, Suite 710, Washington, DC 20036	(202) 349-1155	info@lupus.org	www.lupus.org
MAAP Services for the Autism Spectrum (MAAP)	P.O. Box 524, Crown Point, IN 46308	(219) 662-1311	chart@netnitco.net	www.maapservices.org
MAGIC Foundation	6645 W. North Avenue, Oak Park IL 60302	(708) 383-0808	mary@magicfoundation.org	www.magicfoundation.org
March of Dimes Birth Defects Foundation	1275 Mamaroneck Avenue, White Plains, NY 10605	(914) 428-7100	askus@marchofdimes.com	www.marchofdimes.com
MUMS National Parent-to-Parent Network	150 Custer Ct., Green Bay, WI 54301-1243	(920) 336-5333	mums@netnet.net	www.netnet.net/mums
Muscular Dystrophy Association (MDA)	3300 East Sunrise Drive, Tucson, AZ 85718	(520) 529-2000	mda@mdausa.org	www.mdausa.org
National Alliance for the Mentally Ill (NAMI)	Colonial Place Three, 2107 Wilson Blvd., Suite 300, Arlington, VA 22201-3042	(703) 524-7600	info@nami.org	www.nami.org
National Association for the Dually Diagnosed (NADD)	132 Fair Street, Kingston, NY 12401	(845) 331-4336	info@thenadd.org	www.thenadd.org
National Association of the Deaf	814 Thayer Avenue, Suite 250, Silver Spring, MD 20910	(301) 587-1788	nadinfo@nad.org	www.nad.org

NATIONAL DISABILITY ORGANIZATIONS

ORGANIZATION	ADDRESS	TELEPHONE	EMAIL	WEBSITE
National Association of Hospital Hospitality Houses	P.O. Box 18087, Asheville, NC 28814-0087	(828) 253-1188	helpinghomes@nahhh.org	www.nahhh.org
National Association of Private Special Education Centers (NAPSEC)	1522 K Street N.W., Suite 1032, Washington, DC 20005	(202) 408-3338	napsec@aol.com	www.napsec.com
National Association of Protection and Advocacy Systems (NAPAS)	900 Second Street N.E., Suite 211, Washington, DC 20002	(202) 408-9514	info@napas.org	www.napas.org
National Ataxia Foundation	2600 Fernbrook Lane, Suite 119, Minneapolis, MN 55447	(763) 553-0020	naf@ataxia.org	www.ataxia.org
National Attention Deficit Disorder Association	P.O. Box 543, Pottstown, PA 19464	(484) 944-2101	mail@add.org	www.add.org
National Brain Tumor Foundation	22 Battery Street, Suite 612, San Francisco, CA 94111	(415) 834-9970	nbtf@braintumor.org	www.braintumor.org
National Center for Learning Disabilities (NCLD)	381 Park Avenue South, Suite 1401, New York, NY 10016	(212) 545-7510	help@getreadytoread.org	www.ld.org
National Center for PTSD (Post-Traumatic Stress Disorder)	215 North Main Street, White River Junction, VT 05009	(802) 296-6300	ncptsd@ncptsd.org	www.ncptsd.org
National Center for Special Education Personnel and Related Service Providers	1800 Diagonal Road, Suite 320, Alexandria, VA 22314	(703) 519-3800	none listed	E-mail via website www.personnelcenter.org

How to Protect Your Challenged Child

NATIONAL DISABILITY ORGANIZATIONS

ORGANIZATION	ADDRESS	TELEPHONE	EMAIL	WEBSITE
National Center on Physical Activity and Disability (NCPAD)	1640 W. Roosevelt Road, Chicago, IL 60608-6904	(800) 900-8086	ncpad@uic.edu	www.ncpad.org
National Chronic Fatigue Syndrome and Fibromyalgia Association (NCFSFA)	P.O. Box 18426, Kansas City, MO 64133	(816) 313-2000	information@ncfsfa.org	www.ncfsfa.org
National Council on Independent Living	1916 Wilson Boulevard, Suite 209, Arlington, VA 22201	(703) 525-3406	ncil@ncil.org	www.ncil.org
National Down Syndrome Congress	1370 Center Drive, Suite 102, Atlanta, GA 30338	(770) 604-9500	info@ndsccenter.org	www.ndsccenter.org
National Down Syndrome Society	666 Broadway, 8th Floor, New York, NY 10012-2317	(212) 460-9330	info@ndss.org	ndss.org
National Eating Disorders Association (formerly Eating Disorders Awareness and Prevention)	603 Stewart Street, Suite 803, Seattle, WA 98101	(206) 382-3587	info@NationalEatingDisorders.org	www.nationaleatingdisorders.org
National Federation for the Blind	1800 Johnson Street, Baltimore, MD 21230	(410) 659-9314	nfb@nfb.org	www.nfb.org
National Fragile X Foundation	P.O. Box 190488, San Francisco, CA 94119-0488	(925) 938-9315	NATLFX@FragileX.org	www.fragilex.org
National Gaucher Foundation	5410 Edson Lane, Suite 260, Rockville, MD 20852-3150	(301) 816-1515	ngf@gaucherdisease.org	www.gaucherdisease.org

NATIONAL DISABILITY ORGANIZATIONS

ORGANIZATION	ADDRESS	TELEPHONE	EMAIL	WEBSITE
National Kidney Foundation	30 East 33rd Street, New York, NY 10016	(212) 889-2210	info@kidney.org	www.kidney.org
National Library Service for the Blind & Physically Handicapped	1291 Taylor Street N.W., Washington, DC 20011	(202) 707-5100	nls@loc.gov	www.loc.gov/nls
National Limb Loss Information Center	900 East Hill Avenue, Suite 285, Knoxville, TN 37915-2568	(888) 267-5669	nllicinfo@amputee-coalition.org	www.amputee-coalition.org/nllic_about.html
National Lymphedema Network	1611 Telegraph Avenue, Suite 1111, Oakland, CA 94612	(510) 208-3200	nln@lymphnet.org	www.lymphnet.org
National Mental Health Association	2001 N. Beauregard, 12th Floor, Alexandria VA 22311	(703) 684-7722	E-mail via website.	www.nmha.org
National Mental Health Information Center	P.O. Box 42557, Washington, DC 20015	(800) 789-2647	none listed	www.mentalhealth.org
National Multiple Sclerosis Society	733 Third Avenue, New York, NY 10017	(800) 344-4867	E-mail via website.	www.nationalmssociety.org
National Organization for Albinism and Hypopigmentation (NOAH)	P.O. Box 959, East Hampstead, NH 03826-0959	(603) 887-2310	webmaster@albinism.org	www.albinism.org
National Organization on Disability (NOD)	910 16th Street N.W., Suite 600, Washington, DC 20006	(202) 293-5960	ability@nod.org	www.nod.org

How to Protect Your Challenged Child

NATIONAL DISABILITY ORGANIZATIONS

ORGANIZATION	ADDRESS	TELEPHONE	EMAIL	WEBSITE
National Organization on Fetal Alcohol Syndrome (NOFAS)	900 17th Street NW, Suite 910, Washington, DC 20006	(202) 785-4585	information@nofas.org	www.nofas.org
National Patient Air Transport Hotline	4620 Haygood Road, Suite 1, Virginia Beach, VA 23445	(757) 318-9174	mercymedical@erols.com	www.patienttravel.org
National Resource Center for Family Centered Practice	100 Oakdale Hall, Iowa City, IA 52242-5000	(319) 335-4965	none listed	www.uiowa.edu/~nrcfcp
National Resource Center for Paraprofessionals in Education and Related Services	6526 Old Main Hill, Logan UT 84322-6526	(435) 797-7272	twallace@nrcpara.org	www.nrcpara.org
National Resource Center on Supported Living and Choice	805 S. Crouse Avenue Syracuse, NY 13244-2280	(315) 443-3851	thechp@sued.syr.edu	thechp.syr.edu/nrc.html
National Reye's Syndrome Foundation	P.O. Box 829, Bryan, OH 43506	(419) 636-2679	nrsf@reyessyndrome.org	www.reyessyndrome.org
National Scoliosis Foundation	5 Cabot Place, Stoughton, MA 02072,	(781) 341-6333	NSF@scoliosis.org	www.scoliosis.org
National Sleep Foundation	1522 K Street, N.W., Suite 500, Washington, DC 20005	(202) 347-3471	nsf@sleepfoundation.org	www.sleepfoundation.org

NATIONAL DISABILITY ORGANIZATIONS

ORGANIZATION	ADDRESS	TELEPHONE	EMAIL	WEBSITE
National Spinal Cord Injury Association	6701 Democracy Blvd., Suite 300-9, Bethesda, MD 20817,	(301) 214-4006	info@spinalcord.org	www.spinalcord.org
National Stuttering Association	119 W. 40th Street, 14th Floor, New York, NY 10018	(800) 937-8888	info@westutter.org	www.westutter.org
National Tay-Sachs and Allied Diseases Association	2001 Beacon Street, Suite 204, Brighton, MA 02135	(800) 906-8723	info@ntsad.org	www.ntsad.org
Neurofibromatosis Inc.	9320 Annapolis Road, Suite 300, Lanham, MD 20706-3123	(301) 918-4600	nfinfo@nfinc.org	www.nfinc.org
Nonverbal Learning Disorders Association	2446 Albany Avenue, West Hartford, CT 06117	(800) 570-0217	NLDA@nlda.org	www.nlda.org
Obsessive Compulsive Foundation Inc.	676 State Street, New Haven, CT 06511	(203) 401-2070	info@ocfoundation.org	www.ocfoundation.org
Osteogenesis Imperfecta Foundation	804 Diamond Ave., Suite 210, Gaithersburg, MD 20878	(301) 947-0083	bonelink@oif.org	www.oif.org
Parents Helping Parents: The Parent-Directed Family Resource Center for Children with Special Needs	3041 Olcott St., Santa Clara, CA 95054	(408) 727-5775	info@php.com	www.php.com
Parents of Galactosemic Children	1519 Magnolia Bluff Dr., Gautier, MS 39553	None listed	president@galactosemia.org	www.galactosemia.org

How to Protect Your Challenged Child   111

NATIONAL DISABILITY ORGANIZATIONS

ORGANIZATION	ADDRESS	TELEPHONE	EMAIL	WEBSITE
Pathways Awareness Foundation	150 N. Michigan Avenue, Suite 2100, Chicago, IL 60601	(800) 955-2445	friends@pathwaysawareness.org	www.pathwaysawareness.org
Prader-Willi Syndrome Association	5700 Midnight Pass Road, Suite 6, Sarasota, FL 34242	(941) 312-0400	national@pwsausa.org	www.pwsausa.org

APPENDIX 3:
DSM-IV CRITERIA FOR ATTENTION DEFICIT/HYPERACTIVITY DISORDER

A. According to the DSM-IV, a person with Attention Deficit/Hyperactivity Disorder must have either (1) or (2):

(1) Six (or more) of the following symptoms of inattention have persisted for at least 6 months to a degree that is maladaptive and inconsistent with developmental level:

INATTENTION

(a) often fails to give close attention to details or makes careless mistakes in school work, work, or other activities

(b) often has difficulty sustaining attention in tasks or play activities

(c) often does not seem to listen when spoken to directly

(d) often does not follow through on instructions and fails to finish schoolwork, chores, or duties in the workplace (not due to oppositional behavior or failure to understand instructions)

(e) often has difficulty organizing tasks and activities

(f) often avoids, dislikes, or is reluctant to engage in tasks that require sustained mental effort (such as schoolwork or homework)

(g) often loses things necessary for tasks or activities (e.g., toys, school assignments, pencils, books, or tools)

(h) is often easily distracted by extraneous stimuli

(i) is often forgetful in daily activities

DSM-IV CRITERIA FOR ATTENTION DEFICIT/HYPERACTIVITY DISORDER

(2) Six (or more) of the following symptoms of hyperactivity-impulsivity have persisted for at least 6 months to a degree that is maladaptive and inconsistent with developmental level:

HYPERACTIVITY

(a) often fidgets with hands or feet or squirms in seat

(b) often leaves seat in classroom or in other situations in which remaining seated is expected

(c) often runs about or climbs excessively in situations in which it is inappropriate (in adolescents or adults, may be limited to subjective feelings or restlessness)

(d) often has difficulty playing or engaging in leisure activities quietly

(e) is often "on the go" or often acts as if "driven by a motor"

(f) often talks excessively

(g) often blurts out answers before questions have been completed

(h) often has difficulty awaiting turn

(i) often interrupts or intrudes on others (e.g., butts into conversations or games)

B. Some hyperactive-impulsive or inattentive symptoms that caused impairment were present before age 7 years.

C. Some impairment from the symptoms is present in two or more settings (e.g., at school and at home).

D. There must be clear evidence of clinically significant impairment in social, academic, or occupational functioning.

E. The symptoms do not occur exclusively during the course of a Pervasive Developmental Disorder, Schizophrenia, or other Psychotic Disorder and are not better accounted for by another mental disorder (e.g., Mood Disorder, Anxiety Disorder, Disassociative Disorder, or a Personality Disorder).

ATTENTION DEFICIT/HYPERACTIVITY DISORDER, COMBINED TYPE:

If both Criteria A1 and A2 are met for the past 6 months.

ATTENTION DEFICIT/HYPERACTIVITY DISORDER, PREDOMINANTLY INATTENTIVE TYPE:

If Criterion A1 is met but Criterion A2 is not met for the past 6 months.

ATTENTION DEFICIT/HYPERACTIVITY DISORDER, PREDOMINANTLY HYPERACTIVE-IMPULSIVE TYPE:

If Criterion A2 is met but Criterion A1 is not met for the past 6 months.

Source: American Psychiatric Association: Diagnostic and Statistical Manual of Mental Disorders, Fourth Edition.

APPENDIX 4: CHILD DEVELOPMENT CHECKLIST—BIRTH TO 4 YEARS OF AGE

BIRTH TO THREE MONTHS OLD

Lift his head and chest when on his stomach

Move her arms and her legs easily

Follow your movements by turning his head side to side

Easily take a bottle or breast and suck well

Startle or cry at sudden loud noises

Look at you, watch your face

Make gurgling or cooing sounds

Smile in response to your smile or talk

Quiet easily when comforted

THREE TO SIX MONTHS OLD

Play with his feet when on his back

Lift her head and chest with her weight on hands when on her stomach

Hold her head upright and steady without support

Roll from stomach to back and back to stomach

Play with his own hands by touching them together

Reach for a toy

Pick up a toy placed within reach

Turn his head toward sounds

Make lots of different sounds

Laugh out loud
Begin to show likes and dislikes

SIX TO TWELVE MONTHS OLD
Pull himself to stand with some help
Sit without help while playing with toys
Transfer objects from one hand to the other
Feed herself finger food
Imitate waving bye-bye
Let you know his needs with motions and sounds
Copy speech sounds (ba-ba/ga-ga)
Take turns while playing with adult
Let you know he understands a simple question
Know parents from strangers

TWELVE TO EIGHTEEN MONTHS OLD
Walk alone
Pick up small objects
Put objects into and dump them from containers
Put one object on top of another
Feed himself with spoon
Hold and drink from a cup with some spilling
Point to several things or pictures when named
Say two or three different words in addition to "Mama" or "Dada"
Ask for things using words

EIGHTEEN MONTHS TO TWO YEARS OLD
Walk up and down stairs with his hand held
Scribble
Move her body in time to music
Put two words together
Begin to ask questions
Feed himself a sandwich; taking bites

CHILD DEVELOPMENT CHECKLIST—BIRTH TO 4 YEARS OF AGE

Take off socks and shoes
Look at storybook pictures with an adult
Make simple choices among toys
Mimic another child's play

TWO TO THREE YEARS OLD

Walk well, run, stop, step up, and squat down
Stack more than two objects
Use the spoon and cup all by herself
Follow two-step directions
Name five to six body parts on himself
Take part in simple conversation
Answer simple "what" and "what do" questions
Point to or name objects when told their use
Help with simple tasks
Use 2-3 word sentences regularly

THREE TO FOUR YEARS OLD

Jump, run, throw, climb, using good balance
Draw up, down, around, and sideways using a crayon
Use materials and toys to make things
Enjoy picture books and being read to
Understand words that tell where things are
Use speech that is easily understood
Ask a lot of "why" and "what" questions
Enjoy playing with other children
Wait his turn some of the time
Answer simple "where" and "who" questions

Source: Washington Birth to Six State Planning Project

APPENDIX 5:
DIRECTORY OF STATE SPECIAL EDUCATION AGENCIES

STATE	DEPARTMENT	ADDRESS	TELEPHONE	FAX
ALABAMA	Alabama Department of Education, Division of Special Education Services	50 North Ripley Street, Gordon Persons Building, Montgomery, AL 36130-3901	334-242-8114	334-242-9192
ALASKA	Alaska Department of Education, Office of Special & Supplemental Services	801 West Tenth Street, Suite 200, Juneau, AK 99801-1894	907-465-2971	907-465-3396
ARIZONA	Arizona Department of Education, Special Education Office	1535 West Jefferson, Phoenix, AZ 85007-3280	602-542-3084	602-542-5404
ARKANSAS	Arkansas Department of Education, Special Education Office	State Capitol Mall, Room 105-C #4, Little Rock, AR 72201-1071	501-682-4221	501-682-4313

DIRECTORY OF STATE SPECIAL EDUCATION AGENCIES

STATE	DEPARTMENT	ADDRESS	TELEPHONE	FAX
CALIFORNIA	California Department of Education, Special Education Office	515 L Street, #270, Sacramento, CA 95814	916-445-4602	916-327-3706
COLORADO	Colorado Department of Education, Special Education Services Unit	201 East Colfax Avenue, Denver, CO 80203	303-866-6697	303-866-6811
CONNECTICUT	Connecticut State Department of Education, Bureau of Special Education & Pupil Personnel Services	25 Industrial Park Road, Middletown, CT 06457	860-638-4000	860-638-4156
DISTRICT OF COLUMBIA	D.C. State Office of Special Education	Goding School, 10th and F Streets NE, Washington, DC 20002	202-724-7833	202-724-5116
DELAWARE	Delaware Department of Public Instruction, Exceptional Children Team	PO Box 1402 Dover, DE 19903-1402,	302-739-5471	302-739-2388
FLORIDA	Florida Department of Education, Bureau for Exceptional Students, Florida Education Center	325 West Gaines Street, Suite 614, Tallahassee, FL 32399-0400	904-488-1570	904-487-2194
GEORGIA	Georgia Department of Education, Division for Exceptional Students	1952 Twin Towers East, 205 Butler Street, Atlanta, GA 39334-5040	404-656-3963	404-651-6457
HAWAII	Hawaii Department of Education, Special Education Section	3430 Leahi Avenue, Honolulu, HI 96815	808-733-4990	808-773-4841

DIRECTORY OF STATE SPECIAL EDUCATION AGENCIES

STATE	DEPARTMENT	ADDRESS	TELEPHONE	FAX
IDAHO	Idaho State Department of Education, Special Education Section	650 West State Street, Boise, ID 83720-3650	208-334-3940	208-334-4664
ILLINOIS	Illinois State Board of Education, Center on Policy, Planning and Resource Management	Mail Code E-284, 100 North First Street, Springfield, IL 62777-0001	217-782-3371	217-524-7784
INDIANA	Indiana Department of Education, Division of Special Education	State House, Room 229, Indianapolis, IN 46204-2798	317-232-0570	317-232-0589
IOWA	Iowa Department of Public Instruction, Bureau of Special Education,	Grimes State Office Building, Des Moines, IA 50319-0146	515-281-3176	515-242-6019
KANSAS	Kansas State Board of Education, Special Education Outcomes Team	120 SE 10th Avenue, Topeka, KS 66612-1182	913-296-3869	913-296-7933
KENTUCKY	Kentucky Department of Education, Division of Exceptional Children Services	500 Mero Street, Room 805, Frankfort, KY 40601	502-564-4970	502-564-6721
LOUISIANA	Louisiana Department of Education, Office of Special Education Services	P.O. Box 94064, 9th Floor, Baton Rouge, LA 70804-9064	504-342-3633	504-342-5880
MARYLAND	Maryland Department of Education, Division of Special Education	200 West Baltimore Street, Baltimore, MD 21201-2595	410-767-0238	410-333-8165

DIRECTORY OF STATE SPECIAL EDUCATION AGENCIES

STATE	DEPARTMENT	ADDRESS	TELEPHONE	FAX
MAINE	Maine Department of Education, Division of Special Education	Station #23, Augusta, ME 04333	207-287-5950	207-287-5900
MASSACHUSETTS	Massachusetts Department of Education, Educational Improvement Group	350 Main Street, Malden, MA 02148-5023	617-388-3300	617-388-3394
MICHIGAN	Michigan Department of Education, Special Education Services	P.O. Box 30008, Lansing, MI 48909-75208	517-373-9433	517-373-7504
MINNESOTA	Minnesota Department of Education, Special Education Section	812 Capitol Square Building, 550 Cedar Street, St Paul, MN 55101-2233	612-296-1793	612-297-7368
MISSISSIPPI	Mississippi State Department of Education, Bureau of Special Services	P.O. Box 771, Jackson, MS 39205-0771	601-359-3490	601-359-2326
MISSOURI	Missouri Department of Elementary & Secondary Education, Special Education Programs	P.O. Box 480, Jefferson City, MO 65102-0480	573-751-2965	573-526-4404
MONTANA	Montana Office of Public Instruction, Division of Special Education	State Capitol, Room 106, Helena, MT 59620	406-444-4429	406-444-3924
NEBRASKA	Nebraska Department of Education, Special Education Office	301 Centennial Mall South, P.O. Box 94987, Lincoln, NE 68509-4987	402-471-2471	402-471-0117

DIRECTORY OF STATE SPECIAL EDUCATION AGENCIES

STATE	DEPARTMENT	ADDRESS	TELEPHONE	FAX
NEVADA	Nevada Department of Education, Special Education Branch	440 West King, Capitol Complex, Carson City, NV 89710-0004	702-687-9142	702-687-9123
NEW HAMPSHIRE	New Hampshire Department of Education, Special Education Services	101 Pleasant Street, Concord, NH 03301-3860	603-271-6693	603-271-1953
NEW JERSEY	New Jersey Department of Education	Office of Special Education Programs, CN 500, Trenton, NJ 08625-0001	609-633-6833	609-984-8422
NEW MEXICO	New Mexico State Department of Education, Special Education Department	300 Don Gaspar Avenue, Santa FE, NM 87501-2786	505-827-6541	505-827-6791
NEW YORK	New York State Education Department, Office for Special Education Services	One Commerce Plaza, Room 1901, 99 Washington Avenue, Albany, NY 12234-0001	518-474-5548	518-473-5387
NORTH CAROLINA	North Carolina Department of Public Instruction, Division of Exceptional Childrens Services	301 North Wilmington Street, Raleigh, NC 27601-2825	919-715-1565	919-715-1569
NORTH DAKOTA	North Dakota Department of Public Instruction, Special Education Department	600 East Boulevard, Bismarck, ND 58505-0440	701-328-2277	701-328-2461
OHIO	Ohio Department of Education, Division of Special Education	933 High Street, Worthington, OH 43085-4087	614-466-2650	614-728-1097

DIRECTORY OF STATE SPECIAL EDUCATION AGENCIES

STATE	DEPARTMENT	ADDRESS	TELEPHONE	FAX
OKLAHOMA	Oklahoma State Department of Education, Special Education Section	2500 North Lincoln Boulevard, Oklahoma City, OK 73105-4599	405-521-4868	405-522-3503 John
OREGON	Oregon Department of Education, Office of Special Education	255 Capitol Street NE, Salem, OR 97310-0203	503-378-3598	503-373-7968
PENNSYLVANIA	Pennsylvania Department of Education, Bureau of Special Education	333 Market Street, Harrisburg, PA 17126-0333	717-783-6913	717-783-6139
RHODE ISLAND	Rhode Island Department of Education, Office of Special Needs	Shepard Building, 225 Westminster Street, Providence, RI 02903	401-277-3505	401-277-6030
SOUTH CAROLINA	South Carolina State Department of Education	Office of Programs for Exceptional Children, Rutledge Building, Room 505, 1429 Senate, Columbia, SC 29201	803-734-8806	803-734-4824
SOUTH DAKOTA	South Dakota Department of Education & Cultural Affairs, Office of Special Education	700 Governors Drive, Pierre, SD 57501-2291	605-773-3315	605-773-6139
TENNESSEE	Tennessee Department of Education, Division of Special Education, Gateway Plaza	710 James Robertson Parkway, 8th Floor, Nashville, TN 37243-0380	615-741-2851	615-532-9412
TEXAS	Texas Education Agency, Special Education Unit	Room 5-120, 1701 North Congress Avenue, Austin, TX 78701-2486	512-463-9414	512-463-9838

DIRECTORY OF STATE SPECIAL EDUCATION AGENCIES

STATE	DEPARTMENT	ADDRESS	TELEPHONE	FAX
UTAH	Utah State Office of Education, Special Education Services Unit	250 East 500 South, Salt Lake City, UT 84111-3204	801-538-7711	801-538-7991
VERMONT	Vermont Department of Education, Division of Special Education	120 State Street, State Office Building Montpelier, VT 05602-2501	802-828-5118	802-828-3140
VIRGINIA	Virginia Department of Education, Special Education Department	P.O. Box 2120, Richmond, VA 23216-2120	804-225-2402	804-371-8796
WEST VIRGINIA	West Virginia Department of Education, Office of Special Education	Capitol Complex, 1800 Kanawha Boulevard, Building 6, Room B-304, Charleston, WV 25305	304-558-2696	304-558-3741
WISCONSIN	Wisconsin Department of Public Instruction, Division Learning Support: Equity & Advocacy	125 South Webster, P.O. Box 7841, Madison, WI 53707-7841	608-266-1649	608-267-3746
WYOMING	Wyoming Department of Education, Special Education Unit	Hathaway Building, 2nd Floor, 2300 Capitol Avenue, Cheyenne, WY 82002-0050	307-777-7417	307-777-6234
WASHINGTON	Washington Superintendent of Public Instruction, Special Education Section	Old Capitol Building, Olympia, WA 98504-0001	360-753-6733	360-586-0247

How to Protect Your Challenged Child

APPENDIX 6:
COMPULSORY SCHOOL ATTENDANCE, BY STATE AND AGE

STATE	AGE
Alabama	7 to 16
Alaska	7 to 16
Arizona	6 to 16
Arkansas	5 to 17
California	6 to 18
Colorado	7 to 16
Connecticut	7 to 16
Delaware	5 to 16
District of Columbia	5 to 18
Florida	6 to 18
Georgia	6 to 16
Hawaii	6 to 18
Idaho	7 to 16
Illinois	7 to 16
Indiana	7 to 18
Iowa	6 to 16
Kansas	7 to 18
Kentucky	6 to 16
Louisiana	7 to 17
Maine	7 to 17
Maryland	5 to 16
Massachusetts	6 to 16
Michigan	6 to 16

COMPULSORY SCHOOL ATTENDANCE, BY STATE AND AGE

STATE	AGE
Minnesota	7 to 18
Mississippi	6 to 17
Missouri	7 to 16
Montana	7 to 16
Nebraska	7 to 16
Nevada	7 to 17
New Hampshire	6 to 16
New Jersey	6 to 16
New Mexico	5 to 18
New York	6 to 16
North Carolina	7 to 16
North Dakota	7 to 16
Ohio	6 to 18
Oklahoma	5 to 18
Oregon	7 to 18
Pennsylvania	8 to 17
Rhode Island	6 to 16
South Carolina	5 to 16
South Dakota	6 to 16
Tennessee	6 to 17
Texas	6 to 18
Utah	6 to 18
Vermont	7 to 16
Virginia	5 to 18
Washington	8 to 18
West Virginia	6 to 16
Wisconsin	6 to 18
Wyoming	6 to 16

Source: U.S. Department of Labor

APPENDIX 7:
COMPULSORY SPECIAL EDUCATION SERVICES FOR STUDENTS, BY STATE AND AGE

STATE	AGE
Alabama	6 to 21
Alaska	3 to 22
Arizona	3 to 22
Arkansas	5 to 21
California	Birth to 21
Colorado	3 to 21
Connecticut	Under 21
Delaware	3 to 20
District of Columbia	n/a
Florida	n/a
Georgia	Under 21
Hawaii	Under 20
Idaho	3 to 21
Illinois	3 to 212
Indiana	3 to 22
Iowa	Under 21
Kansas	School age
Kentucky	Under 21
Louisiana	3 to 21
Maine	5 to 19
Maryland	Under 21
Massachusetts	3 to 21

COMPULSORY SPECIAL EDUCATION SERVICES FOR STUDENTS, BY STATE AND AGE

STATE	AGE
Michigan	Under 26
Minnesota	Under 22
Mississippi	Birth to 20
Missouri	Under 21
Montana	3 to 18
Nebraska	Birth to 21
Nevada	Under 22
New Hampshire	3 to 21
New Jersey	5 to 21
New Mexico	School age or as provided by law
New York	Under 21
North Carolina	5 to 20
North Dakota	3 to 20
Ohio	Under 22
Oklahoma	3 and up
Oregon	3 to 21
Pennsylvania	6 to 21
Rhode Island	3 to 21
South Carolina	3 to 21
South Dakota	Under 21
Tennessee	3 ti 21
Texas	3 to 21
Utah	3 to 22
Vermont	3 to 21
Virginia	2 to 21
Washington	3 to 21
West Virginia	5 to 21
Wisconsin	Under 21
Wyoming	3 to 21

NOTES:

1. n/a = not available

Source: Council of Chief State School Officers

APPENDIX 8:
SAMPLE INDIVIDUALIZED EDUCATION PROGRAM

Student Name [space to write]

Date of Meeting to Develop or Review IEP [space to write]

Present Levels of Educational Performance [space to write]

Measurable Annual Goals (Including Benchmarks or Short-Term Objectives) [space to write]

Special Education and Related Services [space to write]

    Start Date [space to write]

    Location [space to write]

    Frequency [space to write]

    Duration [space to write]

Supplementary Aids and Services [space to write]

    Start Date [space to write]

    Location [space to write]

    Frequency [space to write]

    Duration [space to write]

Program Modifications or Supports for School Personnel [space to write]

    Start Date [space to write]

    Location [space to write]

    Frequency [space to write]

    Duration [space to write]

Explanation of Extent, if Any, to Which Child Will Not Participate with Nondisabled Children [space to write]

SAMPLE INDIVIDUALIZED EDUCATION PROGRAM

Administration of State and District-wide Assessments of Student Achievement

Any Individual Modifications In Administration Needed For Child To Participate In State Or District-wide Assessment(s) [space to write]

If IEP Team Determines That Child Will Not Participate In A Particular State Or District-Wide Assessment

    Why isn't the assessment appropriate for the child? [space to write]

    How will the child be assessed? [space to write]

How Child's Progress Toward Annual Goals Will Be Measured [space to write]

How Child's Parents Will Be Regularly Informed Of Child's Progress Toward Annual Goals And Extent To Which Child's Progress Is Sufficient To Meet Goals By End of Year [space to write]

(Beginning at age 16 or younger if determined appropriate by IEP team) Statement of Needed Transition Services, Including, If Appropriate, Statement Of Interagency Responsibilities Or Any Needed Linkages [space to write]

[In a state that transfers rights to the student at the age of majority, the following information must be included beginning at least one year before the student reaches the age of majority]: The student has been informed of the rights under Part B of IDEA, if any, that will transfer to the student on reaching the age of majority [box to check]

NOTE: For each student with a disability beginning at age 14 (or younger, if appropriate), a statement of the student's transition service needs must be included under the applicable parts of the IEP. The statement must focus on the courses the student needs to take to reach his or her post-school goals.

Source: U.S. Education Department>

APPENDIX 9:
SPECIAL EDUCATION INFORMATION RESOURCES

AGENCY	ADDRESS	TELEPHONE	WEBSITE
Office of Special Education Programs	U.S. Department of Education, Mary E. Switzer Building, 330 C Street SW, Washington, DC 20202	(202) 205-5507	www.ed.gov/about/offices/list/osers/osep/
National Information Center for Children and Youth with Disabilities (NICHCY)	P.O. Box 1492, Washington, DC 20013	(800) 695-0285	www.nichcy.org
ERIC Clearinghouse on Disabilities and Gifted Education (ERICEC)	1920 Association Drive, Reston, VA 20191-1589	(800) 328-0272	ericec.org
Technical Assistance for Parent Centers—the Alliance	PACER Center, 4826 Chicago Avenue South, Minneapolis, MN 55417-1098	(888) 248-0822	www.taalliance.org
The Council for Exceptional Children	1920 Association Drive, Reston, VA 20191-1589	(888) 232-7733	www.ideapractices.org

SPECIAL EDUCATION INFORMATION RESOURCES

AGENCY	ADDRESS	TELEPHONE	WEBSITE
Families and Advocates Partnerships for Education (FAPE)	PACER Center, 4826 Chicago Avenue South, Minneapolis, MN 55417-1098	(888) 248-0822	www.fape.org
National Association of State Directors of Special Education	1800 Diagonal Road, Suite 320, Alexandria, VA 22314	(703) 519-3800	www.nasdse.org

Source: U.S. Education Department

APPENDIX 10:
DIRECTORY OF ATTORNEYS WHO REPRESENT PARENTS OF CHILDREN WITH DISABILITIES

STATE	FIRM	ADDRESS	TELEPHONE	FAX
ARIZONA	Jerri Katzerman, Arizona Center for Disability Law	3839 N. Third St., #209, Phoenix, AZ 85012	602-274-6284	602-274-6779
CALIFORNIA	John M. Bayne, Jr., Sole Practitioner	12400 Wilshire Blvd., #400, Los Angeles, CA 90025-1023	310-390-3600	310-572-0673
CALIFORNIA	Thomas E. Beltran, Sole Practitioner	137 North Larchmont Blvd, #256, Los Angeles, CA 90004	213-467-0702	818-891-5070
CALIFORNIA	Allison B. Brightman/Donna R. Levin	Brightman & Levin 1125 Lindero Canyon Rd., #A8, Westlake Village, CA 91362	818-889-898	818-889-8689
CALIFORNIA	Michael S. Cochrane, Sole Practitioner	12315 Oak Knoll Rd., #110, Poway, CA 92064	858-486-3699	858-486-3299

ATTORNEYS WHO REPRESENT PARENTS OF CHILDREN WITH DISABILITIES

STATE	FIRM	ADDRESS	TELEPHONE	FAX
CALIFORNIA	Rene Thomas Folse, Miller and Folse	101 Moody Ct., Thousand Oaks, CA 91361	805-497-0857	805-495-2684
CALIFORNIA	Eric B. Freedus, Frank and Freedus	APC 1202 Kettner Blvd., #6000, San Diego, CA 92101	619-239-3000	619-236-0217
CALIFORNIA	Rich Kitchens, Sole Practitioner	4418 Water Oak Court, Concord, CA 94521	925-687-0143	925-687-0143
CALIFORNIA	Nancy J. LoDolce, Sole Practitioner	411 Russell Ave., Santa Rosa, CA 95403	707-544-4600	N/A
CALIFORNIA	Kathleen M. Loyer, Sole Practitioner	940 Calle Amanecer, Suite L, San Clemente, CA 92673	949-369-1082	949-498-2958
CALIFORNIA	Gary F. Redenbacher, Sole Practitioner	5610 Scotts Valley Drive, #35, Santa Cruz, CA 95066	831-439-8821	831-438-3121
CALIFORNIA	Jane F. Reid, Sole Practitioner	121A North Main Street, Sebastopol, CA 95472	707-824-1466	707-874-2718
CALIFORNIA	Scott C. Van Soye, Sole Practitioner	1920 E. 17th St., Santa Ana, CA 92705-8626	714-835-3090	714-571-3993
CALIFORNIA	Valerie Vanaman, Newman, Aaronson, & Vanaman	14001 Ventura Blvd., Sherman Oaks, CA 91423-3558	818-990-7722	818-501-1306
CALIFORNIA	Bob N. Varma/Geralyn M. Clancy, Varma & Clancy	910 Florin Rd., #212, Sacramento, CA 95831	916-429-4080	916-429-4085
COLORADO	Bradley M. Bittan, Law Office of Bradley M. Bittan	10940 South Parker Rd. #473, Parker, CO 80134	303-805-3543	303-841-1659

ATTORNEYS WHO REPRESENT PARENTS OF CHILDREN WITH DISABILITIES

STATE	FIRM	ADDRESS	TELEPHONE	FAX
COLORADO	Jack D. Robinson, Spies, Powers & Robinson	1660 Lincoln St., #2220, Denver, CO 80264	303-830-7090	303-830-7089
COLORADO	Susan M. Weiner, Law Office of Susan M. Weiner	4450 Arapahoe Ave., #100, Boulder, CO 80303	303-415-2564	303-444-1038
CONNECTICUT	Lawrence D. Church, Sole Practitioner	120 East Ave., Norwalk, CT 06852	203-853-4999	203-853-9429
CONNECTICUT	Howard Klebanoff, Howard Klebanoff, P.C.	433 South Main St., #102, West Hartford, CT 06110	860-313-5005	860-313-5010
CONNECTICUT	Ann A. Nevel, Sole Practitioner	161 Paper Mill Rd., New Milford, CT 06776	860-354-6780	860-355-7144
CONNECTICUT	Winona W. Zimberlin, Sole Practitioner	2 Congress St., Hartford, CT 06114-1024	860-249-5291	860-247-4194
DISTRICT OF COLUMBIA	Beth Goodman, Feldesman, Tucker Leifer, Fidell & Bank	2001 L St., N.W., 3d Flr., Washington, DC 20036-4910	202-466-8960	202-293-8103
DISTRICT OF COLUMBIA	Margaret A. Kohn Kohn & Einstein	1320 19th St., N.W., #200, Washington, DC 20036	202-667-2330	202-667-2302
DISTRICT OF COLUMBIA	James R. Marsh/Sara Dorsch The Children's Law Center Inc.	717 D St., N.W., #210, Washington, DC 20004-2807	202-783-9404	202-783-9403
DISTRICT OF COLUMBIA	Jerrold D. Miller Miller & Miller	1990 M St., N.W., #760, Washington, DC 20036	202-785-2720	202-775-8519

ATTORNEYS WHO REPRESENT PARENTS OF CHILDREN WITH DISABILITIES

STATE	FIRM	ADDRESS	TELEPHONE	FAX
DISTRICT OF COLUMBIA	Travis A. Murrel Murrell & Brown	1401 I St., N.W., #250, Washington, DC 20005	202-289-9001	202-290-9094
FLORIDA	S. James Rosenfeld The EDLAW Center	P.O. Box 81-7327, Hollywood, FL 33081-0327	954-966-4489	561-375-0885
FLORIDA	Joseph Nathaniel Baron Law Office of J.N. Baron, P.A.	P.O. Drawer 1088, Lakeland, FL 33802-1088	941-687-1755	941-687-389
FLORIDA	Michael L. Boswell Michael L. Boswell, P.A.	1009 East Highway 436, Altamonte Springs, FL 32701	407-831-1231	407-831-5813
FLORIDA	Eric Hightower, Davis, Gordon & Doner, P.A.	515 N. Flagler Dr., #700, West Palm Beach, FL 33401	561-659-7337	561-659-0143
FLORIDA	Mark S. Kamleiter, Sole Practitioner	600 First Ave. N., #206, St. Petersburg, FL 33701-3609	813-824-8989	813-824-6389
FLORIDA	Doris Landis Raskin, Sole Practitioner	P.O. Box 1667, Stuart, FL 34995	561-221-2173	561-221-3561
FLORIDA	Joshua H. Rosen Joshua H. Rosen, Chartered	4370 S. Tamiami Trail, #324, Sarasota, FL 34231	941-921-7111	941-927-6616
FLORIDA	Leslie C. Scott Sheppard, White and Thomas, P.A.	215 Washington St., Jacksonville, FL 32202	904-356-9661	904-356-9667
GEORGIA	Dawn R. Smith Zimring, Smith & Billips, P.C.	615 Peachtree St., N.E., #1100, Atlanta, GA 30308	404-607-1600	404-607-1355

ATTORNEYS WHO REPRESENT PARENTS OF CHILDREN WITH DISABILITIES

STATE	FIRM	ADDRESS	TELEPHONE	FAX
GEORGIA	Torin D. Togut Georgia Legal Services Program,	1100 Spring St., #200-A, Atlanta, GA 30309-2848	404-206-5175	404-206-5346
HAWAII	Shelby Anne Floyd Alston, Hunt, Floyd & Ing	1001 Bishop St., 18th Flr., Honolulu, HI 96813	808-524-1800	808-524-4591
HAWAII	Keith H.S. Peck Peck & Associate	1511 Nuuanu Ave., PH #3, Honolulu, HI 96817	808-545-7595	N/A
HAWAII	Arnold T. Phillips II Phillips, Kinkley & Cox	1001 Bishop St., #1250, Honolulu, HI 96813	808-521-8770	808-521-9715
ILLINOIS	Margie Best Law Offices of Margie Best	One North LaSalle St., #2200, Chicago, IL 60602	312-263-4040	312-263-1022
ILLINOIS	Barry D. Bright, Sole Practitioner	P.O. Box 603, Flora, IL 62839	618-662-9585	618-662-7220
ILLINOIS	Matthew Cohen Monahan & Cohen	225 West Washington, #2300, Chicago, IL 60606	312-419-0252	312-419-7428
ILLINOIS	John W. Gaffney Weisz & Michling	2030 North Seminary Ave., Woodstock, IL 60098	815-338-3838	815-338-7817
ILLINOIS	Deborah W. Owens, Sole Practitioner	120 E. Ogden Ave., Ste. 8, Hinsdale, IL 60521	630-789-5856	630-789-9503
ILLINOIS	Miriam F. Solo, Sole Practitioner	6334 N. Whipple, #2B Chicago IL 60659	773-973-3143	773-465-5821
IOWA	Iowa P & A	3015 Merle Hay Rd., #6, Des Moines, IA 50310	515-278-2502	515-278-0539

How to Protect Your Challenged Child

ATTORNEYS WHO REPRESENT PARENTS OF CHILDREN WITH DISABILITIES

STATE	FIRM	ADDRESS	TELEPHONE	FAX
KANSAS	Dwight A. Corrin, Sole Practitioner	P.O. Box 47828, Wichita, KS 67201-7828	316-263-9706	316-263-6385
KANSAS	Peter John Orsi Law Office of Peter John Orsi	610 North Tyler Rd., Wichita, KS 67212	316-729-8825	316-729-8771
KANSAS	Alan R. Post, Sole Practitioner	1803 N. Siefkin St., Wichita, KS 67208-1758	316-686-8232	316-686-8248
KENTUCKY	C. David Emerson/ Robert C. Welleford Emerson & Associates	501 Darby Creek, Unit 41, Lexington, KY 40509	606-264-1664	606-264-1670
MAINE	Richard L. O'Meara Murray, Plumb & Murray	75 Pearl St., Portland, ME 04104-5085	207-773-5651	207-773-8023
MARYLAND	Jeanne Asherman Law Offices of J. Asherman	9015 Walden Rd., Silver Spring, MD 20901	301-587-6990	301-587-6680
MARYLAND	Philip A. Guzman, Sole Practitioner	The Metropolitan Bldg., 8720 Georgia Ave., #706, Silver Spring, MD 20910	301-587-5285	301-565-9391
MARYLAND	Patrick J. Hoover Patrick J. Hoover Law Offices	600 Jefferson Plaza, #308, Rockville, MD 20852	301-424-5777	301-217-9297
MARYLAND	Beth A. Jackson, Sole Practitioner	3454 Ellicott Center Drive, #203, Ellicott City, MD 21043	410-465-8904	410-465-0168
MARYLAND	Mark B. Martin, Sole Practitioner	207 E. Redwood St., #703, Baltimore, MD 21202	410-779-7770	410-576-9391

ATTORNEYS WHO REPRESENT PARENTS OF CHILDREN WITH DISABILITIES

STATE	FIRM	ADDRESS	TELEPHONE	FAX
MARYLAND	Walter D. McQuie, Sole Practitioner	346 Glebe Rd. Easton, MD 21601	410-820-6441	410-763-9312
MARYLAND	Robert H. Plotkin Law Office of Robert H. Plotkin	113 North Washington St., #320, Rockville, MD 20850	301-279-7387	301-279-0386
MARYLAND	Laura N. Venezia, Sole Practitioner	1317 Orchard Way, Frederick, MD 21703	301-694-5530	N/A
MASSACHUSETTS	Glenn Everett Churchill Churchill Law Associates	189 Flagler Drive, Marshfield, MA 02050-2842	781-837-2183	781-834-2061
MASSACHUSETTS	Heather Gold Eckert, Seamans, Cherin & Mellot, LLC	One International Place, 18th Flr., Boston, MA 02110	617-342-6800	617-342-6899
MASSACHUSETTS	Robert K. Crabtree/Lawrence Kotin/Richard Howard/Eileen Hagerty Kotin, Crabtree & Strong, LLP	One Bowdoin Square, Boston, MA 02114-2919	617-227-7031	617-367-2988
MASSACHUSETTS	Kenneth J. Gogel Gogel Law Office	34 Depot St., Pittsfield, MA 01201	413-442-8803	413-443-3461
MASSACHUSETTS	E. Alexandra Golden, Sole Practitioner	175 Highland Ave., Needham, MA 02494	781-433-8665	781-444-8706
MASSACHUSETTS	Carol E. Kervick, Sole Practitioner	21 Concord St., Charlestown, MA 02129	617-242-3458	617-242-3458

How to Protect Your Challenged Child   143

ATTORNEYS WHO REPRESENT PARENTS OF CHILDREN WITH DISABILITIES

STATE	FIRM	ADDRESS	TELEPHONE	FAX
MASSACHUSETTS	John-Paul LaPre, Law Offices of John-Paul LaPre	111 Lakeside Ave., Marlborough, MA 01752	508-481-5505	508-481-4415
MASSACHUSETTS	Geraldine ten Brinke, Sole Practitioner	10 Concord Rd., Sudbury, MA 01776	978-443-9005	978-443-0543
MICHIGAN	John F. Brower, Law Office of John F. Brower	121 West North St., #5, Brighton, MI 48116	810-227-9797	810-227-7996
MICHIGAN	Richard J. Landau, Dykema Gossett, PLLC	315 E. Eisenhower Pkwy., #100, Ann Arbor, MI 48108	734-214-7669	734-214-7696
MICHIGAN	Don L. Rosenberg, Barron & Rosenberg, P.C.	200 East Long Lake Rd., #180, Bloomfield Hills, MI 48304-2361	248-647-4440	248-647-4727
MICHIGAN	Annette E. Skinner, Sole Practitioner	509 E. Grand River Ave., Suite A, Lansing, MI 48906	517-484-7820	517-474-7824
MINNESOTA	Thomas B. James, Sole Practitioner	440 N. Broadway Ave., Cokato, MN 55321	320-286-6425	320-286-6425
MINNESOTA	Sonja D. Kerr, Kerr Law Offices	5972 Cahill Ave., #110, Inver Grove Heights, MN 55076	651-552-4900	651-552-4942
NEVADA	Thomas J. Moore, Sole Practitioner	2810 W. Charleston Blvd., #F-62, Las Vegas, NV 89102	702-593-9556	702-870-1029
NEW JERSEY	Penelope A. Boyd, Law Offices of Penelope A. Boyd	000 Atrium Way, #292, Mt. Laurel, NJ 08054	609-273-3142	609-273-6913

ATTORNEYS WHO REPRESENT PARENTS OF CHILDREN WITH DISABILITIES

STATE	FIRM	ADDRESS	TELEPHONE	FAX
NEW JERSEY	John M. Capasso, Sole Practitioner	1230 Shore Rd. Linwood, NJ 08221	609-926-9288	609-926-2288
NEW JERSEY	Jamie Epstein, Sole Practitioner	38 West End Ave., Haddonfield, NJ 08033	609-354-8008	609-354-8008
NEW JERSEY	Carole Ann Geronimo, Sole Practitioner	1 DeMercurio Drive, Allendale, NJ 07401	201-512-4400	201-512-4403
NEW JERSEY	Herbert D. Hinkle/Linda R. Robinson Law Offices of Herbert D. Hinkle	2651 Main St., #A, Lawrenceville, NJ 08648	609-896-4200	609-895-9524
NEW JERSEY	George M. Holland Williams, Caliri, Miller & Otley	1428 Route 23, Wayne, NJ 07474	201-694-0800	201-694-0302
NEW JERSEY	Harriet W. Rothfeld, Sole Practitioner	225 Millburn Ave., #206, Millburn, NJ 07041-1712	201-376-7373	201-376-3847
NEW JERSEY	Philip D. Stern, Sole Practitioner	225 Millburn Ave., #208, Millburn, NJ 07041-1712	201-912-9393	201-912-4343
NEW JERSEY	Theodore A. Sussan/ Staci J. Greenwald Sussan and Greenwald,	407 Main St., Spotswood, NJ 08884	732-251-8585	732-238-0900
NEW YORK	Charles G. Davis Esq. Davis and Davis	20 Squadron Blvd. #350, New City, NY	914-634-6633	914-634-7688
NEW YORK	Michael E. Deffet Leon & Deffet	235 Brooksite Drive, Hauppauge, NY 11788	516-360-6694	516-361-7324

ATTORNEYS WHO REPRESENT PARENTS OF CHILDREN WITH DISABILITIES

STATE	FIRM	ADDRESS	TELEPHONE	FAX
NEW YORK	Barbara J. Ebenstein, Ebenstein & Ebenstein	801 Second Ave., #1402, New York, NY 10017	212-687-4433	212-687-4436
NEW YORK	Sami Kahn, Sole Practitioner	305 Broadway, #500, New York, NY 10007	212-577-6877	N/A
NEW YORK	Deborah R. Monheit, Sole Practitioner	P.O. Box 163, East Setauket, N.Y. 11773	516-751-6070	516-651-6512
NEW YORK	Neal H. Rosenberg, Law Offices of Neal H. Rosenberg	9 Murray St., #7W, New York, NY 10007-228	212-732-9450	212-732-4443
NEW YORK	Robert Testino, Sole Practitioner	91 Columbia St., Albany, NY 12210	518-426-4667	518-462-3826
NORTH CAROLINA	Edward J. Bedford, Pinna, Johnston, O'Donoghue & Burwell, P.A.	P.O. Box 31788, Raleigh, NC 27622	919-755-1317	919-782-0452
NORTH CAROLINA	Barbara Jackson, Holt & York, LLP	P.O. Box 17105, Raleigh, NC 27619	919-420-7826	919-420-7838
OHIO	Franklin J. Hickman/Janet L. Lowder/Melody L. Harness, Hickman & Lowder Co., LPA	1370 Ontario St., #1620, Cleveland, OH 44113-1743	216-861-0360	216-861-3113
OHIO	Lisa B. Avirov, Sole Practitioner	8070 Beechmont Ave., #4, Cincinnati, OH 45255	513-474-4466	513-474-5800
OHIO	Michael E. Deffet, Leon & Deffet	P.O. Box 458, Phillipsburg, OH 45354	937-884-5540	937-884-5540

ATTORNEYS WHO REPRESENT PARENTS OF CHILDREN WITH DISABILITIES

STATE	FIRM	ADDRESS	TELEPHONE	FAX
OHIO	Ohio State Legal Services Association	N/A 861 North High St., Columbus, OH 43215	614-299-2114	614-299-6364
OHIO	Nessa G. Siegel Nessa G. Siegel Co. Inc.	4070 Mayfield Rd. Cleveland, OH 44121	216-291-1300	216-291-9622
OKLAHOMA	Moura A.J. Robertson McCormick, Schoenenberger & Robertson, P.A.	1441 South Carson Ave., Tulsa, OK 74119-3417	918-582-3655	918-582-3657
OKLAHOMA	Mary J. Rounds Mary J. Rounds P.C.	406 South Boulder Ave., #400, Tulsa, OK 74103	918-592-1900	918-592-0928
OREGON	David A. Bahr Bahr & Stotter Law Offices	259 E. Fifth Ave., #200, Eugene, OR 97401	541-686-3277	541-686-2137
OREGON	Mary E. Broadhurst Mary E. Broadhurst P.C.	P.O. Box 11377, Eugene, OR 97440	541-683-8530	541-687-9767
OREGON	Dana R. Taylor Hagen Dye, Hirschy & DiLorenzo, P.C.	One S.W. Columbia St., #1900, Portland, OR 97258	503-222-1812	503-274-7979
PENNSYLVANIA	Penelope A. Boyd Law Offices of Penelope A. Boyd	101 Breesey Court, 517 East Lancaster Ave., Downington, PA 19335	610-873-6939	610-518-0349
PENNSYLVANIA	Paul J. Drucker Law Offices Bernard M. Gross P.C.	1500 Walnut St., 6th Flr., Philadelphia, PA 19102	215-561-3600	215-561-3000

ATTORNEYS WHO REPRESENT PARENTS OF CHILDREN WITH DISABILITIES

STATE	FIRM	ADDRESS	TELEPHONE	FAX
PENNSYVANIA	J. Lawrence Hajduk/Mary L. Hajduk/Mark A. Rowan/Leslie Crosco J. Lawrence Hajduk & Associates	5340 National Pike, Markleysburg, PA 15459	412-329-1133	412-329-8959
PENNSYLVANIA	Herbert D. Hinkle Law Offices of Herbert D. Hinkle	2651 Main St., #A, Lawrenceville, NJ 08648	215-860-2100	609-895-9524
PENNSYLVANIA	Yvonne M. Husic Nicholas & Foreman, P.C.	4409 North Front St., Harrisburg, PA 17110-1709	717-236-9391	717-236-6602
PENNSYLVANIA	Elizabeth Kapo, Sole Practitioner	34 N. Fifth St., Allentown, PA 18101	610-770-7399	610-770-6909
PENNSYLVANIA	Vivian B. Narehood Gibbel Kraybill & Hess	41 East Orange St., Lancaster, PA 17602	717-291-1700	717-291-5547
PENNSYLVANIA	Philip Matthew Stinson, Sr Stinson Law Associates, P.C.	895 Glenbrook Ave., Bryn Mawr, PA 19010-7340	610-519-0390	610-519-0394
PUERTO RICO	Wilfredo A. Ruiz W. A. Ruiz Law Offices	#49 Hiram Gonzalez St., Bayamon, PR 00959	787-787-2122	787-787-2302
RHODE ISLAND	Melissa A. Korpacz Korpacz & Associates	13 Dickinson Ave., #3, North Providence, RI 02904	401-723-0069	N/A
RHODE ISLAND	Richard D. Pass Pass Law Associates	1445 Wampanoag Trail, #115, East Providence, RI 02915	401-433-1414	401-433-1692

ATTORNEYS WHO REPRESENT PARENTS OF CHILDREN WITH DISABILITIES

STATE	FIRM	ADDRESS	TELEPHONE	FAX
SOUTH DAKOTA	Robert J. Kean/John A. Hamilton/Lynne A. Valenti	South Dakota Advocacy Services 221 S. Central Ave. Pierre, SD 57501-2453	605-224-8294	605-224-5125
TEXAS	C. Michael Black Law Office of C. Michael Black	2444 Times Blvd., #222, Houston, TX 77005	713-522-5999	713-522-2625
TEXAS	Chris Jonas, Sole Practitioner	3349 Jamaica Dr., Corpus Christi, TX 78418	361-937-1801	361-937-1802
TEXAS	David Aaron Piña Lopez, Piña & Urrutia	611 South Congress, #340, Austin, TX 78704	512-442-7299	512-326-3171
TEXAS	Advocacy, Inc.	7800 Shoal Creek Blvd., #142-S, Austin, TX 78757-1024	512-454-4816	512-323-0902
UTAH	David G. Challed Challed Law Offices	254 West 400 South, #320, Salt Lake City, UT 84101	801-355-3500	801-359-6873
VIRGINIA	Frank M. Feibelman Hill, Rainey & Eliades	731 W. Broadway, P.O. Box 1007, Hopewell, VA 23860-1007	804-541-1941	804-541-5602
VIRGINIA	Barbara S. Jenkins Jenkins & Hagy, PLC	401 Ridge St., Charlottesville, VA 22902	804-296-4998	804-296-9647
VIRGINIA	Lois N. Manes, Sole Practitioner	P.O. Box 1675, Williamsburg, VA 23187	757-229-6224	757-220-8515
VIRGINIA	Peter W.D. Wright, Sole Practitioner	P.O. Box 1008 Deltaville, VA 23043-1008	804-776-7008	N/A

How to Protect Your Challenged Child

ATTORNEYS WHO REPRESENT PARENTS OF CHILDREN WITH DISABILITIES

STATE	FIRM	ADDRESS	TELEPHONE	FAX
WASHINGTON	Steven N. Bogdon Blair, Schaefer, Hutchison & Wolfe, LLP	105 W. Evergreen Blvd., P.O. Box 1148, Vancouver, WA 98666-1148	360-693-5883	360-693-1777
WASHINGTON	William L.E. Dussaul, Sole Practitioner	219 East Galer St., Seattle, WA 98102-3794	206-324-4300	206-324-3106
WASHINGTON	Larry A. Jones, Sole Practitioner	2118 8th Ave., Seattle, WA 98121	206-405-3240	206-405-3243
WASHINGTON	Edward L. Lane, Sole Practitioner	607 SW Grady Way, #110, Renton WA 98055	425-226-1418	425-226-1246
WASHINGTON	Mary E. McKnew, Sole Practitione	7840 Warbler Ct., SE, Olympia, WA 98513	360-459-0554	360-459-0359
WEST VIRGINIA	William F. Byrne Byrne & Hedge	141 Walnut St., Morgantown, WV 26505	304-296-0123	304-296-0713
WEST VIRGINIA	Robert J. O'Brien, Sole Practitioner	43 S. Florida St., Buckhannon, WV 26201	304-472-2456	304-472-2456

Source: EDLAW Inc. (http://www.edlaw.net/attylist.html)

APPENDIX 11: SELECTED PROVISIONS OF SECTION 504 OF THE REHABILITATION ACT OF 1973 (29 U.S.C. 794)

TITLE 29

CHAPTER 16—VOCATIONAL REHABILITATION AND OTHER REHABILITATION SERVICES

SUBCHAPTER V—RIGHTS AND ADVOCACY

Section 794. Nondiscrimination under Federal grants and programs

(a) Promulgation of rules and regulations

No otherwise qualified individual with a disability in the United States, as defined in section 706(8) of this title, shall, solely by reason of her or his disability, be excluded from the participation in, be denied the benefits of, or be subjected to discrimination under any program or activity receiving Federal financial assistance or under any program or activity conducted by any Executive agency or by the United States Postal Service. The head of each such agency shall promulgate such regulations as may be necessary to carry out the amendments to this section made by the Rehabilitation, Comprehensive Services, and Developmental Disabilities Act of 1978. Copies of any proposed regulation shall be submitted to appropriate authorizing committees of the Congress, and such regulation may take effect no earlier than the thirtieth day after the date on which such regulation is so submitted to such committees.

SECTION 504 OF THE REHABILITATION ACT OF 1973

(b) "Program or activity" defined

For the purposes of this section, the term "program or activity" means all of the operations of 0151

>(1)(A) a department, agency, special purpose district, or other instrumentality of a State or of a local government; or
>
>(B) the entity of such State or local government that distributes such assistance and each such department or agency (and each other State or local government entity) to which the assistance is extended, in the case of assistance to a State or local government;
>
>(2)(A) a college, university, or other postsecondary institution, or a public system of higher education; or
>
>(B) a local educational agency (as defined in section 8801 of title 20), system of vocational education, or other school system.

Section 794a. Remedies and attorney fees

(b) In any action or proceeding to enforce or charge a violation of a provision of this subchapter, the court, in its discretion, may allow the prevailing party, other than the United States, a reasonable attorney's fee as part of the costs.

Section 794c. Interagency Disability Coordinating

(a) Establishment

There is hereby established an Interagency Disability Coordinating Council (hereafter in this section referred to as the "Council") composed of the Secretary of Education, the Secretary of Health and Human Services, the Secretary of Labor, the Secretary of Housing and Urban Development, the Secretary of Transportation, the Assistant Secretary of the Interior for Indian Affairs, the Attorney General, the Director of the Office of Personnel Management, the Chairperson of the Equal Employment Opportunity Commission, the Chairperson of the Architectural and Transportation Barriers Compliance Board, and such other officials as may be designated by the President.

(b) Duties

The Council shall—

>(1) have the responsibility for developing and implementing agreements, policies, and practices designed to maximize effort, promote efficiency, and eliminate conflict, competition, duplication, and inconsistencies among the operations, functions, and jurisdictions of the various departments, agencies, and branches of the Federal Government responsible for the implementation and enforcement of the

provisions of this subchapter, and the regulations prescribed thereunder;

(2) be responsible for developing and implementing agreements, policies, and practices designed to coordinate operations, functions, and jurisdictions of the various departments and agencies of the Federal Government responsible for promoting the full integration into society, independence, and productivity of individuals with disabilities; and

(3) carry out such studies and other activities, subject to the availability of resources, with advice from the National Council on Disability, in order to identify methods for overcoming barriers to integration into society, independence, and productivity of individuals with disabilities.

(c) Report

On or before July 1 of each year, the Interagency Disability Coordinating Council shall prepare and submit to the President and to the Congress a report of the activities of the Council designed to promote and meet the employment needs of individuals with disabilities, together with such recommendations for legislative and administrative changes as the Council concludes are desirable to further promote this section, along with any comments submitted by the National Council on Disability as to the effectiveness of such activities and recommendations in meeting the needs of individuals with disabilities. Nothing in this section shall impair any responsibilities assigned by any Executive order to any Federal department, agency, or instrumentality to act as a lead Federal agency with respect to any provisions of this subchapter.

Section 794d. Electronic and information technology accessibility guidelines

(a) Guidelines

The Secretary, through the Director of the National Institute on Disability and Rehabilitation Research, and the Administrator of the General Services Administration, in consultation with the electronics and information technology industry and the Interagency Council on Accessible Technology, shall develop and establish guidelines for Federal agencies for electronic and information technology accessibility designed to ensure, regardless of the type of medium, that individuals with disabilities can produce information and data, and have access to information and data, comparable to the information and data, and access, respectively, of individuals who are not individuals with disabilities. Such guidelines shall be revised, as necessary, to reflect technological advances or changes.

SECTION 504 OF THE REHABILITATION ACT OF 1973

(b) Compliance

Each Federal agency shall comply with the guidelines established under this section.

APPENDIX 12: SELECTED PROVISIONS OF THE INDIVIDUALS WITH DISABILITIES EDUCATION ACT (20 U.S.C. 33)

SUBCHAPTER I—GENERAL PROVISIONS

Section 1400. Congressional Findings and Purpose.

(a) Short Title.

This chapter may be cited as the "Individuals with Disabilities Education Act."

(b) Findings.

The Congress finds the following:

(1) Disability is a natural part of the human experience and in no way diminishes the right of individuals to participate in or contribute to society. Improving educational results for children with disabilities is an essential element of our national policy of ensuring equality of opportunity, full participation, independent living, and economic self-sufficiency for individuals with disabilities.

(2) Before the date of the enactment of the Education for All Handicapped Children Act of 1975 (Public Law 94-142)—

(A) the special educational needs of children with disabilities were not being fully met;

(B) more than one-half of the children with disabilities in the United States did not receive appropriate educational services that would enable such children to have full equality of opportunity;

(C) 1,000,000 of the children with disabilities in the United States were excluded entirely from the public school system and did not go through the educational process with their peers;

INDIVIDUALS WITH DISABILITIES EDUCATION ACT

(D) there were many children with disabilities throughout the United States participating in regular school programs whose disabilities prevented such children from having a successful educational experience because their disabilities were undetected; and

(E) because of the lack of adequate services within the public school system, families were often forced to find services outside the public school system, often at great distance from their residence and at their own expense.

(3) Since the enactment and implementation of the Education for All Handicapped Children Act of 1975, this Act has been successful in ensuring children with disabilities and the families of such children access to a free appropriate public education and in improving educational results for children with disabilities.

(c) Purposes.

The purposes of this title are—

(1)(A) to ensure that all children with disabilities have available to them a free appropriate public education that emphasizes special education and related services designed to meet their unique needs and prepare them for employment and independent living;

(B) to ensure that the rights of children with disabilities and parents of such children are protected; and

(C) to assist States, localities, educational service agencies, and Federal agencies to provide for the education of all children with disabilities;

(2) to assist States in the implementation of a statewide, comprehensive, coordinated, multidisciplinary, interagency system of early intervention services for infants and toddlers with disabilities and their families;

(3) to ensure that educators and parents have the necessary tools to improve educational results for children with disabilities by supporting systemic-change activities; coordinated research and personnel preparation; coordinated technical assistance, dissemination, and support; and technology development and media services; and

(4) to assess, and ensure the effectiveness of, efforts to educate children with disabilities.

Section 1402. Office of Special Education Programs.

(a) Establishment.

There shall be, within the Office of Special Education and Rehabilitative Services in the Department of Education, an Office of Special Education Programs, which shall be the principal agency in such Department for administering and carrying out this Act and other programs and activities concerning the education of children with disabilities.

(b) Director.

The Office established under subsection (a) shall be headed by a Director who shall be selected by the Secretary and shall report directly to the Assistant Secretary for Special Education and Rehabilitative Services.

(c) Voluntary and Uncompensated Services.

Notwithstanding section 1342 of title 31, United States Code, the Secretary is authorized to accept voluntary and uncompensated services in furtherance of the purposes of this Act.

Section 1403. Abrogation of State Sovereign Immunity.

(a) In General.

A State shall not be immune under the eleventh amendment to the Constitution of the United States from suit in Federal court for a violation of this Act.

(b) Remedies.

In a suit against a State for a violation of this Act, remedies (including remedies both at law and in equity) are available for such a violation to the same extent as those remedies are available for such a violation in the suit against any public entity other than a State.

(c) Effective Date.

Subsections (a) and (b) apply with respect to violations that occur in whole or part after the date of the enactment of the Education of the Handicapped Act Amendments of 1990.

SUBCHAPTER II—ASSISTANCE FOR EDUCATION OF ALL CHILDREN WITH DISABILITIES

Section 1411. Authorization; Allotment; Use of Funds; Authorization of Appropriations.

(1) Free Appropriate Public Education.

(A) In General. A free appropriate public education is available to all children with disabilities residing in the State between the ages of 3 and 21, inclusive, including children with disabilities who have been suspended or expelled from school.

(B) Limitation. The obligation to make a free appropriate public education available to all children with disabilities does not apply with respect to children:

(i) aged 3 through 5 and 18 through 21 in a State to the extent that its application to those children would be inconsistent with State law or practice, or the order of any court, respecting the provision of public education to children in those age ranges; and

(ii) aged 18 through 21 to the extent that State law does not require that special education and related services under this part be provided to children with disabilities who, in the educational placement prior to their incarceration in an adult correctional facility:

(I) were not actually identified as being a child with a disability under Section 1402(3) of this Act; or

(II) did not have an individualized education program under this part.

(2) Full Educational Opportunity Goal. The State has established a goal of providing full educational opportunity to all children with disabilities and a detailed timetable for accomplishing that goal.

(3) Child Find.

(A) In General. All children with disabilities residing in the State, including children with disabilities attending private schools, regardless of the severity of their disabilities, and who are in need of special education and related services, are identified, located, and evaluated and a practical method is developed and implemented to determine which children with disabilities are currently receiving needed special education and related services.

(B) Construction. Nothing in this Act requires that children be classified by their disability so long as each child who has a disability listed in Section 1402 and who, by reason of that disability, needs special education and related services is regarded as a child with a disability under this part.

(4) Individualized Education Program. An individualized education program, or an individualized family service plan that meets the requirements of Section 1436(d), is developed, reviewed, and revised for each child with a disability in accordance with Section 1414(d).

(5) Least Restrictive Environment.

(A) In General. To the maximum extent appropriate, children with disabilities, including children in public or private institutions or other care facilities, are educated with children who are not disabled, and special classes, separate schooling, or other removal of children with disabilities from the regular educational environment occurs only when the nature or severity of the disability of a child is such that education in regular classes with the use of supplementary aids and services cannot be achieved satisfactorily.

(B) Additional Requirement.

(i) In General. If the State uses a funding mechanism by which the State distributes State funds on the basis of the type of setting in which a child is served, the funding mechanism does not result in placements that violate the requirements of subparagraph (A).

(ii) Assurance. If the State does not have policies and procedures to ensure compliance with clause (i), the State shall provide the Secretary an assurance that it will revise the funding mechanism as soon as feasible to ensure that such mechanism does not result in such placements.

(6) Procedural Safeguards.

(A) In General. Children with disabilities and their parents are afforded the procedural safeguards required by Section 1415.

(B) Additional Procedural Safeguards. Procedures to ensure that testing and evaluation materials and procedures utilized for the purposes of evaluation and placement of children with disabilities will be selected and administered so as not to be racially or culturally discriminatory. Such materials or procedures shall be provided and administered in the child's native language or mode of communication, unless it clearly is not feasible to do so, and no single procedure shall be the sole criterion for determining an appropriate educational program for a child.

(7) Evaluation. Children with disabilities are evaluated in accordance with subsections (a) through (c) of Section 1414.

(8) Confidentiality. Agencies in the State comply with Section 1417(c) (relating to the confidentiality of records and information).

(9) Transition From Part C to Preschool Programs. Children participating in early-intervention programs assisted under part C, and who will participate in preschool programs assisted under this part, experience a smooth and effective transition to those preschool programs in a manner consistent with Section 1437(a)(8). By the third birthday of such a child, an individualized education program or, if consistent with sections 1414(d)(2)(B) and 1436(d), an individualized family service plan, has been developed and is being implemented for the child. The local educational agency will participate in transition planning conferences arranged by the designated lead agency under Section 1437(a)(8).

(10) Children in Private Schools.

   (A) Children Enrolled in Private Schools by Their Parents.

      (i) In General. To the extent consistent with the number and location of children with disabilities in the State who are enrolled by their parents in private elementary and secondary schools, provision is made for the participation of those children in the program assisted or carried out under this part by providing for such children education and related services in accordance with the following requirements, unless the Secretary has arranged for services to those children under subsection (f):

         (I) Amounts expended for the provision of those services by a local educational agency shall be equal to a proportionate amount of Federal funds made available under this part.

         (II) Such services may be provided to children with disabilities on the premises of private, including parochial, schools, to the extent consistent with law.

      (ii) Child-find Requirement. The requirements of paragraph (3) of this subsection (relating to child find) shall apply with respect to children with disabilities in the State who are enrolled in private, including parochial, elementary and secondary schools.

   (B) Children Placed in, or Referred to, Private Schools by Public Agencies.

      (i) In General. Children with disabilities in private schools and facilities are provided special education and related services, in accordance with an individualized education program, at no cost to their parents, if such children are placed in, or referred to, such schools or facilities by the State or appropriate local educational agency as the means of carrying out the requirements of this part or any other applicable law requiring the provision of special education and related services to all children with disabilities within such State.

(ii) Standards. In all cases described in clause (i), the State educational agency shall determine whether such schools and facilities meet standards that apply to State and local educational agencies and that children so served have all the rights they would have if served by such agencies.

(C) Payment for Education of Children Enrolled in Private Schools without Consent of or Referral by the Public Agency.

(i) In General. Subject to subparagraph (A), this part does not require a local educational agency to pay for the cost of education, including special education and related services, of a child with a disability at a private school or facility if that agency made a free appropriate public education available to the child and the parents elected to place the child in such private school or facility.

(ii) Reimbursement for Private School Placement. If the parents of a child with a disability, who previously received special education and related services under the authority of a public agency, enroll the child in a private elementary or secondary school without the consent of or referral by the public agency, a court or a hearing officer may require the agency to reimburse the parents for the cost of that enrollment if the court or hearing officer finds that the agency had not made a free appropriate public education available to the child in a timely manner prior to that enrollment.

(iii) Limitation On Reimbursement. The cost of reimbursement described in clause (ii) may be reduced or denied—

(I) if—

(aa) at the most recent IEP meeting that the parents attended prior to removal of the child from the public school, the parents did not inform the IEP Team that they were rejecting the placement proposed by the public agency to provide a free appropriate public education to their child, including stating their concerns and their intent to enroll their child in a private school at public expense;

(bb) 10 business days (including any holidays that occur on a business day) prior to the removal of the child from the public school, the parents did not give written notice to the public agency of the information described in division (aa);

(II) if, prior to the parents' removal of the child from the public school, the public agency informed the parents, through the notice requirements described in Section 1415(b)(7), of its intent to evaluate the child (including a statement of the purpose of the evaluation that was appropriate and reasonable), but the parents did not make the child available for such evaluation; or

(III) upon a judicial finding of unreasonableness with respect to actions taken by the parents.

(iv) Exception. Notwithstanding the notice requirement in clause (iii)(I), the cost of reimbursement may not be reduced or denied for failure to provide such notice if—

(I) the parent is illiterate and cannot write in English;

(II) compliance with clause (iii)(I) would likely result in physical or serious emotional harm to the child;

(III) the school prevented the parent from providing such notice; or

(IV) the parents had not received notice, pursuant to Section 1415, of the notice requirement in clause (iii)(I).

(11) State Educational Agency Responsible for General Supervision.

(A) In General. The State educational agency is responsible for ensuring that—

(i) the requirements of this part are met; and

(ii) all educational programs for children with disabilities in the State, including all such programs administered by any other State or local agency—

(I) are under the general supervision of individuals in the State who are responsible for educational programs for children with disabilities; and

(II) meet the educational standards of the State educational agency.

(B) Limitation. Subparagraph (A) shall not limit the responsibility of agencies in the State other than the State educational agency to provide, or pay for some or all of the costs of, a free appropriate public education for any child with a disability in the State.

(15) Personnel Standards.

(A) In General. The State educational agency has established and maintains standards to ensure that personnel necessary to carry out this part are appropriately and adequately prepared and trained.

(C) Policy. In implementing this paragraph, a State may adopt a policy that includes a requirement that local educational agencies in the State make an ongoing good-faith effort to recruit and hire appropriately and adequately trained personnel to provide special education and related services to children with disabilities, including, in a geographic area of the State where there is a shortage of such personnel, the most qualified individuals available who are making satisfactory progress toward completing applicable course work necessary to meet the standards described in subparagraph (B)(i), consistent with State law, and the steps described in subparagraph (B)(ii) within three years.

(17) Participation in Assessments.

(A) In General. Children with disabilities are included in general State and district-wide assessment programs, with appropriate accommodations, where necessary. As appropriate, the State or local educational agency—

(i) develops guidelines for the participation of children with disabilities in alternate assessments for those children who cannot participate in State and district-wide assessment programs; and

(ii) develops and, beginning not later than July 1, 2000, conducts those alternate assessments.

(19) Maintenance of State Financial Support.

(A) In General. The State does not reduce the amount of State financial support for special education and related services for children with disabilities, or otherwise made available because of the excess costs of educating those children, below the amount of that support for the preceding fiscal year.

(B) Reduction of Funds for Failure to Maintain Support. The Secretary shall reduce the allocation of funds under Section 1411 for any fiscal year following the fiscal year in which the State fails to comply with the requirement of subparagraph (A) by the same amount by which the State fails to meet the requirement.

(C) Waivers for Exceptional or Uncontrollable Circumstances. The Secretary may waive the requirement of subparagraph (A) for a State, for one fiscal year at a time, if the Secretary determines that—

(i) granting a waiver would be equitable due to exceptional or uncontrollable circumstances such as a natural disaster or a precipitous and unforeseen decline in the financial resources of the State; or

(ii) the State meets the standard in paragraph (18)(C) of this section for a waiver of the requirement to supplement, and not to supplant, funds received under this part.

(20) Public Participation. Prior to the adoption of any policies and procedures needed to comply with this section (including any amendments to such policies and procedures), the State ensures that there are public hearings, adequate notice of the hearings, and an opportunity for comment available to the general public, including individuals with disabilities and parents of children with disabilities.

(21) State Advisory Panel.

(A) In General. The State has established and maintains an advisory panel for the purpose of providing policy guidance with respect to special education and related services for children with disabilities in the State.

(B) Membership. Such advisory panel shall consist of members appointed by the Governor, or any other official authorized under State law to make such appointments, that is representative of the State population and that is composed of individuals involved in, or concerned with, the education of children with disabilities, including—

(i) parents of children with disabilities;

(ii) individuals with disabilities;

(iii) teachers;

(iv) representatives of institutions of higher education that prepare special education and related services personnel;

(v) State and local education officials;

(vi) administrators of programs for children with disabilities;

(vii) representatives of other State agencies involved in the financing or delivery of related services to children with disabilities;

(viii) representatives of private schools and public charter schools;

INDIVIDUALS WITH DISABILITIES EDUCATION ACT

(ix) at least one representative of a vocational, community, or business organization concerned with the provision of transition services to children with disabilities; and (x) representatives from the State juvenile and adult corrections agencies.

(C) Special Rule. A majority of the members of the panel shall be individuals with disabilities or parents of children with disabilities.

(D) Duties. The advisory panel shall—

(i) advise the State educational agency of unmet needs within the State in the education of children with disabilities;

(ii) comment publicly on any rules or regulations proposed by the State regarding the education of children with disabilities;

(iii) advise the State educational agency in developing evaluations and reporting on data to the Secretary under Section 1418;

(iv) advise the State educational agency in developing corrective action plans to address findings identified in Federal monitoring reports under this part; and

(v) advise the State educational agency in developing and implementing policies relating to the coordination of services for children with disabilities.

Section 1413. Local Educational Agency Eligibility.

(a) In General.

A local educational agency is eligible for assistance under this part for a fiscal year if such agency demonstrates to the satisfaction of the State educational agency that it meets each of the following conditions:

(1) Consistency with State Policies. The local educational agency, in providing for the education of children with disabilities within its jurisdiction, has in effect policies, procedures, and programs that are consistent with the State policies and procedures established under Section 1412.

(2) Use of Amounts.

(A) In General. Amounts provided to the local educational agency under this part shall be expended in accordance with the applicable provisions of this part and—

(i) shall be used only to pay the excess costs of providing special education and related services to children with disabilities;

(ii) shall be used to supplement State, local, and other Federal funds and not to supplant such funds; and

(iii) shall not be used, except as provided in subparagraphs (B) and (C), to reduce the level of expenditures for the education of children with disabilities made by the local educational agency from local funds below the level of those expenditures for the preceding fiscal year.

(6) Additional Requirements.

(A) Parental Involvement. In carrying out the requirements of this subsection, a local educational agency shall ensure that the parents of children with disabilities are involved in the design, evaluation, and, where appropriate, implementation of school-based improvement plans in accordance with this subsection.

(j) Disciplinary Information.

The State may require that a local educational agency include in the records of a child with a disability a statement of any current or previous disciplinary action that has been taken against the child and transmit such statement to the same extent that such disciplinary information is included in, and transmitted with, the student records of nondisabled children. The statement may include a description of any behavior engaged in by the child that required disciplinary action, a description of the disciplinary action taken, and any other information that is relevant to the safety of the child and other individuals involved with the child. If the State adopts such a policy, and the child transfers from one school to another, the transmission of any of the child's records must include both the child's current individualized education program and any such statement of current or previous disciplinary action that has been taken against the child.

Section 1414. Evaluations, Eligibility Determinations, Individualized Education Programs, and Educational Placements.

(a) Evaluations and Re-evaluations.

(1) Initial Evaluations.

(A) In General. A State educational agency, other State agency, or local educational agency shall conduct a full and individual initial evaluation, in accordance with this paragraph and subsection (b), before the initial provision of special education and related services to a child with a disability under this part.

(B) Procedures. Such initial evaluation shall consist of procedures—

(i) to determine whether a child is a child with a disability (as defined in Section 1402(3)); and

(ii) to determine the educational needs of such child.

(C) Parental Consent.

(i) In General. The agency proposing to conduct an initial evaluation to determine if the child qualifies as a child with a disability as defined in Section 1402(3)(A) or 602(3)(B) shall obtain an informed consent from the parent of such child before the evaluation is conducted. Parental consent for evaluation shall not be construed as consent for placement for receipt of special education and related services.

(ii) Refusal. If the parents of such child refuse consent for the evaluation, the agency may continue to pursue an evaluation by utilizing the mediation and due process procedures under Section 1415, except to the extent inconsistent with State law relating to parental consent.

(2) Re-evaluations. A local educational agency shall ensure that a reevaluation of each child with a disability is conducted—

(A) if conditions warrant a reevaluation or if the child's parent or teacher requests a reevaluation, but at least once every 3 years; and

(B) in accordance with subsections (b) and (c).

(b) Evaluation Procedures.

(1) Notice. The local educational agency shall provide notice to the parents of a child with a disability, in accordance with subsections (b)(3), (b)(4), and (c) of Section 1415, that describes any evaluation procedures such agency proposes to conduct.

(2) Conduct of Evaluation. In conducting the evaluation, the local educational agency shall—

(A) use a variety of assessment tools and strategies to gather relevant functional and developmental information, including information provided by the parent, that may assist in determining whether the child is a child with a disability and the content of the child's individualized education program, including information related to enabling the child to be involved in and progress in the general curriculum or, for preschool children, to participate in appropriate activities;

(B) not use any single procedure as the sole criterion for determining whether a child is a child with a disability or determining an appropriate educational program for the child; and

(C) use technically sound instruments that may assess the relative contribution of cognitive and behavioral factors, in addition to physical or developmental factors.

(3) Additional Requirements. Each local educational agency shall ensure that—

(A) tests and other evaluation materials used to assess a child under this section—

(i) are selected and administered so as not to be discriminatory on a racial or cultural basis; and

(ii) are provided and administered in the child's native language or other mode of communication, unless it is clearly not feasible to do so; and

(B) any standardized tests that are given to the child—

(i) have been validated for the specific purpose for which they are used;

(ii) are administered by trained and knowledgeable personnel; and

(iii) are administered in accordance with any instructions provided by the producer of such tests;

(C) the child is assessed in all areas of suspected disability; and

(D) assessment tools and strategies that provide relevant information that directly assists persons in determining the educational needs of the child are provided.

(4) Determination of Eligibility. Upon completion of administration of tests and other evaluation materials—

(A) the determination of whether the child is a child with a disability as defined in Section 1402(3) shall be made by a team of qualified professionals and the parent of the child in accordance with paragraph (5); and

(B) a copy of the evaluation report and the documentation of determination of eligibility will be given to the parent.

(5) Special Rule for Eligibility Determination. In making a determination of eligibility under paragraph (4)(A), a child shall not be determined to be a child with a disability if the determinant factor for such determination is lack of instruction in reading or math or limited English proficiency.

(c) Additional Requirements for Evaluation and Re-evaluations.

(1) Review of Existing Evaluation Data. As part of an initial evaluation (if appropriate) and as part of any reevaluation under this section, the

IEP Team described in subsection (d)(1)(B) and other qualified professionals, as appropriate, shall—

(A) review existing evaluation data on the child, including evaluations and information provided by the parents of the child, current classroom-based assessments and observations, and teacher and related services providers observation; and

(B) on the basis of that review, and input from the child's parents, identify what additional data, if any, are needed to determine—

(i) whether the child has a particular category of disability, as described in Section 1402(3), or, in case of a reevaluation of a child, whether the child continues to have such a disability;

(ii) the present levels of performance and educational needs of the child;

(iii) whether the child needs special education and related services, or in the case of a reevaluation of a child, whether the child continues to need special education and related services; and

(iv) whether any additions or modifications to the special education and related services are needed to enable the child to meet the measurable annual goals set out in the individualized education program of the child and to participate, as appropriate, in the general curriculum.

(2) Source of Data. The local educational agency shall administer such tests and other evaluation materials as may be needed to produce the data identified by the IEP Team under paragraph (1)(B).

(3) Parental Consent. Each local educational agency shall obtain informed parental consent, in accordance with subsection (a)(1)(C), prior to conducting any reevaluation of a child with a disability, except that such informed parent consent need not be obtained if the local educational agency can demonstrate that it had taken reasonable measures to obtain such consent and the child's parent has failed to respond.

(4) Requirements If Additional Data Are Not Needed. If the IEP Team and other qualified professionals, as appropriate, determine that no additional data are needed to determine whether the child continues to be a child with a disability, the local educational agency—

(A) shall notify the child's parents of—

(i) that determination and the reasons for it; and

(ii) the right of such parents to request an assessment to determine whether the child continues to be a child with a disability; and

(B) shall not be required to conduct such an assessment unless requested to by the child's parents.

(5) Evaluations Before Change in Eligibility. A local educational agency shall evaluate a child with a disability in accordance with this section before determining that the child is no longer a child with a disability.

(d) Individualized Education Programs.

(1) Definitions. As used in this title:

(A) Individualized Education Program. The term 'individualized education program' or 'IEP' means a written statement for each child with a disability that is developed, reviewed, and revised in accordance with this section and that includes—

(i) a statement of the child's present levels of educational performance, including—

(I) how the child's disability affects the child's involvement and progress in the general curriculum; or

(II) for preschool children, as appropriate, how the disability affects the child's participation in appropriate activities;

(ii) a statement of measurable annual goals, including benchmarks or short-term objectives, related to—

(I) meeting the child's needs that result from the child's disability to enable the child to be involved in and progress in the general curriculum; and

(II) meeting each of the child's other educational needs that result from the child's disability;

(iii) a statement of the special education and related services and supplementary aids and services to be provided to the child, or on behalf of the child, and a statement of the program modifications or supports for school personnel that will be provided for the child

(I) to advance appropriately toward attaining the annual goals;

(II) to be involved and progress in the general curriculum in accordance with clause (i) and to participate in extracurricular and other nonacademic activities; and

(III) to be educated and participate with other children with disabilities and nondisabled children in the activities described in this paragraph;

(iv) an explanation of the extent, if any, to which the child will not participate with nondisabled children in the regular class and in the activities described in clause (iii);

(v)(I) a statement of any individual modifications in the administration of State or districtwide assessments of student achievement that are needed in order for the child to participate in such assessment; and

(II) if the IEP Team determines that the child will not participate in a particular State or districtwide assessment of student achievement (or part of such an assessment), a statement of—

(aa) why that assessment is not appropriate for the child; and

(bb) how the child will be assessed;

(vi) the projected date for the beginning of the services and modifications described in clause (iii), and the anticipated frequency, location, and duration of those services and modifications;

(vii)(I) beginning at age 14, and updated annually, a statement of the transition service needs of the child under the applicable components of the child's IEP that focuses on the child's courses of study (such as participation in advanced-placement courses or a vocational education program);

(II) beginning at age 16 (or younger, if determined appropriate by the IEP Team), a statement of needed transition services for the child, including, when appropriate, a statement of the interagency responsibilities or any needed linkages; and

(III) beginning at least one year before the child reaches the age of majority under State law, a statement that the child has been informed of his or her rights under this title, if any, that will transfer to the child on reaching the age of majority under Section 1415(m); and

(viii) a statement of—

(I) how the child's progress toward the annual goals described in clause (ii) will be measured; and

(II) how the child's parents will be regularly informed (by such means as periodic report cards), at least as often as parents are informed of their nondisabled children's progress, of—

(aa) their child's progress toward the annual goals described in clause (ii); and

(bb) the extent to which that progress is sufficient to enable the child to achieve the goals by the end of the year.

INDIVIDUALS WITH DISABILITIES EDUCATION ACT

(B) Individualized Education Program Team. The term 'individualized education program team' or 'IEP Team' means a group of individuals composed of—

(i) the parents of a child with a disability;

(ii) at least one regular education teacher of such child (if the child is, or may be, participating in the regular education environment);

(iii) at least one special education teacher, or where appropriate, at least one special education provider of such child;

(iv) a representative of the local educational agency who—

(I) is qualified to provide, or supervise the provision of, specially designed instruction to meet the unique needs of children with disabilities;

(II) is knowledgeable about the general curriculum; and

(III) is knowledgeable about the availability of resources of the local educational agency;

(v) an individual who can interpret the instructional implications of evaluation results, who may be a member of the team described in clauses (ii) through (vi);

(vi) at the discretion of the parent or the agency, other individuals who have knowledge or special expertise regarding the child, including related services personnel as appropriate; and

(vii) whenever appropriate, the child with a disability.

(2) Requirement That Program Be in Effect.

(A) In General. At the beginning of each school year, each local educational agency, State educational agency, or other State agency, as the case may be, shall have in effect, for each child with a disability in its jurisdiction, an individualized education program, as defined in paragraph (1)(A).

(B) Program for Child Aged 3 Through 5. In the case of a child with a disability aged 3 through 5 (or, at the discretion of the State educational agency, a 2 year-old child with a disability who will turn age 3 during the school year), an individualized family service plan that contains the material described in Section 1436, and that is developed in accordance with this section, may serve as the IEP of the child if using that plan as the IEP is—

(i) consistent with State policy; and

(ii) agreed to by the agency and the child's parents.

(3) Development of IEP.

    (A) In General. In developing each child's IEP, the IEP Team, subject to subparagraph (C), shall consider—

        (i) the strengths of the child and the concerns of the parents for enhancing the education of their child; and

        (ii) the results of the initial evaluation or most recent evaluation of the child.

    (B) Consideration of Special Factors. The IEP Team shall—

        (i) in the case of a child whose behavior impedes his or her learning or that of others, consider, when appropriate, strategies, including positive behavioral interventions, strategies, and supports to address that behavior;

        (ii) in the case of a child with limited English proficiency, consider the language needs of the child as such needs relate to the child's IEP;

        (iii) in the case of a child who is blind or visually impaired, provide for instruction in Braille and the use of Braille unless the IEP Team determines, after an evaluation of the child's reading and writing skills, needs, and appropriate reading and writing media (including an evaluation of the child's future needs for instruction in Braille or the use of Braille), that instruction in Braille or the use of Braille is not appropriate for the child;

        (iv) consider the communication needs of the child, and in the case of a child who is deaf or hard of hearing, consider the child's language and communication needs, opportunities for direct communications with peers and professional personnel in the child's language and communication mode, academic level, and full range of needs, including opportunities for direct instruction in the child's language and communication mode; and

        (v) consider whether the child requires assistive technology devices and services.

    (C) Requirement with Respect to Regular Education Teacher. The regular education teacher of the child, as a member of the IEP Team, shall, to the extent appropriate, participate in the development of the IEP of the child, including the determination of appropriate positive behavioral interventions and strategies and the determination of supplementary aids and services, program modifications, and support for school personnel consistent with paragraph (1)(A)(iii).

(4) Review and Revision of IEP.

    (A) In General. The local educational agency shall ensure that, subject to subparagraph (B), the IEP Team—

        (i) reviews the child's IEP periodically, but not less than annually to determine whether the annual goals for the child are being achieved; and

        (ii) revises the IEP as appropriate to address—

            (I) any lack of expected progress toward the annual goals and in the general curriculum, where appropriate;

            (II) the results of any reevaluation conducted under this section;

            (III) information about the child provided to, or by, the parents, as described in subsection (c)(1)(B);

            (IV) the child's anticipated needs; or

            (V) other matters.

    (B) Requirement with Respect to Regular Education Teacher. The regular education teacher of the child, as a member of the IEP Team, shall, to the extent appropriate, participate in the review and revision of the IEP of the child.

(5) Failure to Meet Transition Objectives. If a participating agency, other than the local educational agency, fails to provide the transition services described in the IEP in accordance with paragraph (1)(A)(vii), the local educational agency shall reconvene the IEP Team to identify alternative strategies to meet the transition objectives for the child set out in that program.

(f) Educational Placements.

Each local educational agency or State educational agency shall ensure that the parents of each child with a disability are members of any group that makes decisions on the educational placement of their child.

Section 1415. Procedural Safeguards.

(a) Establishment of Procedures.

Any State educational agency, State agency, or local educational agency that receives assistance under this part shall establish and maintain procedures in accordance with this section to ensure that children with disabilities and their parents are guaranteed procedural safeguards with respect to the provision of free appropriate public education by such agencies.

(b) Types of Procedures.

The procedures required by this section shall include—

(1) an opportunity for the parents of a child with a disability to examine all records relating to such child and to participate in meetings with respect to the identification, evaluation, and educational placement of the child, and the provision of a free appropriate public education to such child, and to obtain an independent educational evaluation of the child;

(2) procedures to protect the rights of the child whenever the parents of the child are not known, the agency cannot, after reasonable efforts, locate the parents, or the child is a ward of the State, including the assignment of an individual (who shall not be an employee of the State educational agency, the local educational agency, or any other agency that is involved in the education or care of the child) to act as a surrogate for the parents;

(3) written prior notice to the parents of the child whenever such agency—

(A) proposes to initiate or change; or

(B) refuses to initiate or change; the identification, evaluation, or educational placement of the child, in accordance with subsection (c), or the provision of a free appropriate public education to the child;

(4) procedures designed to ensure that the notice required by paragraph (3) is in the native language of the parents, unless it clearly is not feasible to do so;

(5) an opportunity for mediation in accordance with subsection (e);

(6) an opportunity to present complaints with respect to any matter relating to the identification, evaluation, or educational placement of the child, or the provision of a free appropriate public education to such child;

(7) procedures that require the parent of a child with a disability, or the attorney representing the child, to provide notice (which shall remain confidential)—

(A) to the State educational agency or local educational agency, as the case may be, in the complaint filed under paragraph (6); and

(B) that shall include —

(i) the name of the child, the address of the residence of the child, and the name of the school the child is attending;

(ii) a description of the nature of the problem of the child relating to such proposed initiation or change, including facts relating to such problem; and

(iii) a proposed resolution of the problem to the extent known and available to the parents at the time; and

(8) procedures that require the State educational agency to develop a model form to assist parents in filing a complaint in accordance with paragraph (7).

(c) Content of Prior Written Notice.

The notice required by subsection (b)(3) shall include —

(1) a description of the action proposed or refused by the agency;

(2) an explanation of why the agency proposes or refuses to take the action;

(3) a description of any other options that the agency considered and the reasons why those options were rejected;

(4) a description of each evaluation procedure, test, record, or report the agency used as a basis for the proposed or refused action;

(5) a description of any other factors that are relevant to the agency's proposal or refusal;

(6) a statement that the parents of a child with a disability have protection under the procedural safeguards of this part and, if this notice is not an initial referral for evaluation, the means by which a copy of a description of the procedural safeguards can be obtained; and

(7) sources for parents to contact to obtain assistance in understanding the provisions of this part.

(d) Procedural Safeguards Notice.

(1) In General. A copy of the procedural safeguards available to the parents of a child with a disability shall be given to the parents, at a minimum—

(A) upon initial referral for evaluation;

(B) upon each notification of an individualized education program meeting and upon reevaluation of the child; and

(C) upon registration of a complaint under subsection (b)(6).

(2) Contents. The procedural safeguards notice shall include a full explanation of the procedural safeguards, written in the native language of the parents, unless it clearly is not feasible to do so, and written in

an easily understandable manner, available under this section and under regulations promulgated by the Secretary relating to —

(A) independent educational evaluation;

(B) prior written notice;

(C) parental consent;

(D) access to educational records;

(E) opportunity to present complaints;

(F) the child's placement during pendency of due process proceedings;

(G) procedures for students who are subject to placement in an interim alternative educational setting;

(H) requirements for unilateral placement by parents of children in private schools at public expense;

(I) mediation;

(J) due process hearings, including requirements for disclosure of evaluation results and recommendations;

(K) State-level appeals (if applicable in that State);

(L) civil actions; and

(M) attorneys' fees.

(e) Mediation.

(1) In General. Any State educational agency or local educational agency that receives assistance under this part shall ensure that procedures are established and implemented to allow parties to disputes involving any matter described in subsection (b)(6) to resolve such disputes through a mediation process which, at a minimum, shall be available whenever a hearing is requested under subsection (f) or (k).

(2) Requirements. Such procedures shall meet the following requirements:

(A) The procedures shall ensure that the mediation process—

(i) is voluntary on the part of the parties;

(ii) is not used to deny or delay a parent's right to a due process hearing under subsection (f), or to deny any other rights afforded under this part; and

(iii) is conducted by a qualified and impartial mediator who is trained in effective mediation techniques.

(B) A local educational agency or a State agency may establish procedures to require parents who choose not to use the mediation process to meet, at a time and location convenient to the parents, with a disinterested party who is under contract with—

(i) a parent training and information center or community parent resource center in the State established under Section 1482 or 1483; or

(ii) an appropriate alternative dispute resolution entity;

to encourage the use, and explain the benefits, of the mediation process to the parents.

(C) The State shall maintain a list of individuals who are qualified mediators and knowledgeable in laws and regulations relating to the provision of special education and related services.

(D) The State shall bear the cost of the mediation process, including the costs of meetings described in subparagraph (B).

(E) Each session in the mediation process shall be scheduled in a timely manner and shall be held in a location that is convenient to the parties to the dispute.

(F) An agreement reached by the parties to the dispute in the mediation process shall be set forth in a written mediation agreement.

(G) Discussions that occur during the mediation process shall be confidential and may not be used as evidence in any subsequent due process hearings or civil proceedings and the parties to the mediation process may be required to sign a confidentiality pledge prior to the commencement of such process.

(f) Impartial Due Process Hearing.

(1) In General. Whenever a complaint has been received under subsection (b)(6) or (k) of this section, the parents involved in such complaint shall have an opportunity for an impartial due process hearing, which shall be conducted by the State educational agency or by the local educational agency, as determined by State law or by the State educational agency.

(2) Disclosure of Evaluations and Recommendations.

(A) In General. At least 5 business days prior to a hearing conducted pursuant to paragraph (1), each party shall disclose to all other parties all evaluations completed by that date and recommendations based on the offering party's evaluations that the party intends to use at the hearing.

(B) Failure to Disclose. A hearing officer may bar any party that fails to comply with subparagraph (A) from introducing the relevant evaluation or recommendation at the hearing without the consent of the other party.

(3) Limitation on Conduct of Hearing. A hearing conducted pursuant to paragraph (1) may not be conducted by an employee of the State educational agency or the local educational agency involved in the education or care of the child.

(g) Appeal.

If the hearing required by subsection (f) is conducted by a local educational agency, any party aggrieved by the findings and decision rendered in such a hearing may appeal such findings and decision to the State educational agency. Such agency shall conduct an impartial review of such decision. The officer conducting such review shall make an independent decision upon completion of such review.

(h) Safeguards.

Any party to a hearing conducted pursuant to subsection (f) or (k), or an appeal conducted pursuant to subsection (g), shall be accorded —

(1) the right to be accompanied and advised by counsel and by individuals with special knowledge or training with respect to the problems of children with disabilities;

(2) the right to present evidence and confront, cross-examine, and compel the attendance of witnesses;

(3) the right to a written, or, at the option of the parents, electronic verbatim record of such hearing; and

(4) the right to written, or, at the option of the parents, electronic findings of fact and decisions (which findings and decisions shall be made available to the public consistent with the requirements of Section 1417(c) (relating to the confidentiality of data, information, and records) and shall also be transmitted to the advisory panel established pursuant to Section 1412(a)(21)).

(i) Administrative Procedures.

(1) In General.

(A) Decision Made in Hearing. A decision made in a hearing conducted pursuant to subsection (f) or (k) shall be final, except that any party involved in such hearing may appeal such decision under the provisions of subsection (g) and paragraph (2) of this subsection.

(B) Decision Made at Appeal. A decision made under subsection (g) shall be final, except that any party may bring an action under paragraph (2) of this subsection.

(2) Right to Bring Civil Action.

(A) In General. Any party aggrieved by the findings and decision made under subsection (f) or (k) who does not have the right to an appeal under subsection (g), and any party aggrieved by the findings and decision under this subsection, shall have the right to bring a civil action with respect to the complaint presented pursuant to this section, which action may be brought in any State court of competent jurisdiction or in a district court of the United States without regard to the amount in controversy.

(B) Additional Requirements. In any action brought under this paragraph, the court—

(i) shall receive the records of the administrative proceedings;

(ii) shall hear additional evidence at the request of a party; and

(iii) basing its decision on the preponderance of the evidence, shall grant such relief as the court determines is appropriate.

(3) Jurisdiction of District Courts; Attorneys' Fees.

(A) In General. The district courts of the United States shall have jurisdiction of actions brought under this section without regard to the amount in controversy.

(B) Award of Attorneys' Fees. In any action or proceeding brought under this section, the court, in its discretion, may award reasonable attorneys' fees as part of the costs to the parents of a child with a disability who is the prevailing party.

(C) Determination of Amount of Attorneys' Fees. Fees awarded under this paragraph shall be based on rates prevailing in the community in which the action or proceeding arose for the kind and quality of services furnished. No bonus or multiplier may be used in calculating the fees awarded under this subsection.

(D) Prohibition of Attorneys' Fees and Related Costs for Certain Services.

(i) Attorneys' fees may not be awarded and related costs may not be reimbursed in any action or proceeding under this section for services performed subsequent to the time of a written offer of settlement to a parent if—

(I) the offer is made within the time prescribed by Rule 68 of the Federal Rules of Civil Procedure or, in the case of an admin-

INDIVIDUALS WITH DISABILITIES EDUCATION ACT

istrative proceeding, at any time more than 10 days before the proceeding begins;

(II) the offer is not accepted within 10 days; and

(III) the court or administrative hearing officer finds that the relief finally obtained by the parents is not more favorable to the parents than the offer of settlement.

(ii) Attorneys' fees may not be awarded relating to any meeting of the IEP Team unless such meeting is convened as a result of an administrative proceeding or judicial action, or, at the discretion of the State, for a mediation described in subsection (e) that is prior to the filing of a complaint under subsection (b)(6) or (k) of this section.

(E) Exception to Prohibition on Attorneys' Fees and Related Costs. Notwithstanding subparagraph (D), an award of attorneys' fees and related costs may be made to a parent who is the prevailing party and who was substantially justified in rejecting the settlement offer.

(F) Reduction in Amount of Attorneys' Fees. Except as provided in subparagraph (G), whenever the court finds that —

(i) the parent, during the course of the action or proceeding, unreasonably protracted the final resolution of the controversy;

(ii) the amount of the attorneys' fees otherwise authorized to be awarded unreasonably exceeds the hourly rate prevailing in the community for similar services by attorneys of reasonably comparable skill, reputation, and experience;

(iii) the time spent and legal services furnished were excessive considering the nature of the action or proceeding; or

(iv) the attorney representing the parent did not provide to the school district the appropriate information in the due process complaint in accordance with subsection (b)(7);

the court shall reduce, accordingly, the amount of the attorneys' fees awarded under this section.

(G) Exception to Reduction in Amount of Attorneys' Fees. The provisions of subparagraph (F) shall not apply in any action or proceeding if the court finds that the State or local educational agency unreasonably protracted the final resolution of the action or proceeding or there was a violation of this section.

(j) Maintenance of Current Educational Placement.

Except as provided in subsection (k)(7), during the pendency of any proceedings conducted pursuant to this section, unless the State or local educational agency and the parents otherwise agree, the child shall remain in the then-current educational placement of such child, or, if applying for initial admission to a public school, shall, with the consent of the parents, be placed in the public school program until all such proceedings have been completed.

(k) Placement in Alternative Educational Setting.

(1) Authority of School Personnel.

(A) School personnel under this section may order a change in the placement of a child with a disability—

(i) to an appropriate interim alternative educational setting, another setting, or suspension, for not more than 10 school days (to the extent such alternatives would be applied to children without disabilities); and

(ii) to an appropriate interim alternative educational setting for the same amount of time that a child without a disability would be subject to discipline, but for not more than 45 days if—

(I) the child carries a weapon to school or to a school function under the jurisdiction of a State or a local educational agency; or

(II) the child knowingly possesses or uses illegal drugs or sells or solicits the sale of a controlled substance while at school or a school function under the jurisdiction of a State or local educational agency.

(B) Either before or not later than 10 days after taking a disciplinary action described in subparagraph (A)—

(i) if the local educational agency did not conduct a functional behavioral assessment and implement a behavioral intervention plan for such child before the behavior that resulted in the suspension described in subparagraph (A), the agency shall convene an IEP meeting to develop an assessment plan to address that behavior; or

(ii) if the child already has a behavioral intervention plan, the IEP Team shall review the plan and modify it, as necessary, to address the behavior.

(2) Authority of Hearing Officer. A hearing officer under this section may order a change in the placement of a child with a disability to an appro-

priate interim alternative educational setting for not more than 45 days if the hearing officer—

(A) determines that the public agency has demonstrated by substantial evidence that maintaining the current placement of such child is substantially likely to result in injury to the child or to others;

(B) considers the appropriateness of the child's current placement;

(C) considers whether the public agency has made reasonable efforts to minimize the risk of harm in the child's current placement, including the use of supplementary aids and services; and

(D) determines that the interim alternative educational setting meets the requirements of paragraph (3)(B).

(3) Determination of Setting.

(A) In General. The alternative educational setting described in paragraph (1)(A)(ii) shall be determined by the IEP Team.

(B) Additional Requirements. Any interim alternative educational setting in which a child is placed under paragraph (1) or (2) shall—

(i) be selected so as to enable the child to continue to participate in the general curriculum, although in another setting, and to continue to receive those services and modifications, including those described in the child's current IEP, that will enable the child to meet the goals set out in that IEP; and

(ii) include services and modifications designed to address the behavior described in paragraph (1) or paragraph (2) so that it does not recur.

(4) Manifestation Determination Review.

(A) In General. If a disciplinary action is contemplated as described in paragraph (1) or paragraph (2) for a behavior of a child with a disability described in either of those paragraphs, or if a disciplinary action involving a change of placement for more than 10 days is contemplated for a child with a disability who has engaged in other behavior that violated any rule or code of conduct of the local educational agency that applies to all children—

(i) not later than the date on which the decision to take that action is made, the parents shall be notified of that decision and of all procedural safeguards accorded under this section; and

(ii) immediately, if possible, but in no case later than 10 school days after the date on which the decision to take that action is made, a review shall be conducted of the relationship between the child's disability and the behavior subject to the disciplinary action.

(B) Individuals to Carry Out Review. A review described in subparagraph (A) shall be conducted by the IEP Team and other qualified personnel.

(C) Conduct of Review. In carrying out a review described in subparagraph (A), the IEP Team may determine that the behavior of the child was not a manifestation of such child's disability only if the IEP Team—

(i) first considers, in terms of the behavior subject to disciplinary action, all relevant information, including—

(I) evaluation and diagnostic results, including such results or other relevant information supplied by the parents of the child;

(II) observations of the child; and

(III) the child's IEP and placement; and

(ii) then determines that—

(I) in relationship to the behavior subject to disciplinary action, the child's IEP and placement were appropriate and the special education services, supplementary aids and services, and behavior intervention strategies were provided consistent with the child's IEP and placement;

(II) the child's disability did not impair the ability of the child to understand the impact and consequences of the behavior subject to disciplinary action; and

(III) the child's disability did not impair the ability of the child to control the behavior subject to disciplinary action.

(5) Determination That Behavior Was Not Manifestation of Disability.

(A) In General. If the result of the review described in paragraph (4) is a determination, consistent with paragraph (4)(C), that the behavior of the child with a disability was not a manifestation of the child's disability, the relevant disciplinary procedures applicable to children without disabilities may be applied to the child in the same manner in which they would be applied to children without disabilities, except as provided in Section 1412(a)(1).

(B) Additional Requirement. If the public agency initiates disciplinary procedures applicable to all children, the agency shall ensure that the special education and disciplinary records of the child with a disability are transmitted for consideration by the person or persons making the final determination regarding the disciplinary action.

(6) Parent Appeal.

(A) In General.

(i) If the child's parent disagrees with a determination that the child's behavior was not a manifestation of the child's disability or with any decision regarding placement, the parent may request a hearing.

(ii) The State or local educational agency shall arrange for an expedited hearing in any case described in this subsection when requested by a parent.

(B) Review of Decision.

(i) In reviewing a decision with respect to the manifestation determination, the hearing officer shall determine whether the public agency has demonstrated that the child's behavior was not a manifestation of such child's disability consistent with the requirements of paragraph (4)(C).

(ii) In reviewing a decision under paragraph (1)(A)(ii) to place the child in an interim alternative educational setting, the hearing officer shall apply the standards set out in paragraph (2).

(7) Placement During Appeals.

(A) In General. When a parent requests a hearing regarding a disciplinary action described in paragraph (1)(A)(ii) or paragraph (2) to challenge the interim alternative educational setting or the manifestation determination, the child shall remain in the interim alternative educational setting pending the decision of the hearing officer or until the expiration of the time period provided for in paragraph (1)(A)(ii) or paragraph (2), whichever occurs first, unless the parent and the State or local educational agency agree otherwise.

(B) Current Placement. If a child is placed in an interim alternative educational setting pursuant to paragraph (1)(A)(ii) or paragraph (2) and school personnel propose to change the child's placement after expiration of the interim alternative placement, during the pendency of any proceeding to challenge the proposed change in placement, the child shall remain in the current placement (the child's placement prior to the interim alternative educational setting), except as provided in subparagraph (C).

(C) Expedited Hearing.

(i) If school personnel maintain that it is dangerous for the child to be in the current placement (placement prior to removal to the interim alternative education setting) during the pendency of the due process proceedings, the local educational agency may request an expedited hearing.

(ii) In determining whether the child may be placed in the alternative educational setting or in another appropriate placement ordered by the hearing officer, the hearing officer shall apply the standards set out in paragraph (2).

(8) Protections for Children Not Yet Eligible for Special Education and Related Services.

(A) In General. A child who has not been determined to be eligible for special education and related services under this part and who has engaged in behavior that violated any rule or code of conduct of the local educational agency, including any behavior described in paragraph (1), may assert any of the protections provided for in this part if the local educational agency had knowledge (as determined in accordance with this paragraph) that the child was a child with a disability before the behavior that precipitated the disciplinary action occurred.

(B) Basis of Knowledge. A local educational agency shall be deemed to have knowledge that a child is a child with a disability if—

(i) the parent of the child has expressed concern in writing (unless the parent is illiterate or has a disability that prevents compliance with the requirements contained in this clause) to personnel of the appropriate educational agency that the child is in need of special education and related services;

(ii) the behavior or performance of the child demonstrates the need for such services;

(iii) the parent of the child has requested an evaluation of the child pursuant to Section 1414; or

(iv) the teacher of the child, or other personnel of the local educational agency, has expressed concern about the behavior or performance of the child to the director of special education of such agency or to other personnel of the agency.

(C) Conditions That Apply if No Basis of Knowledge.

(i) In General. If a local educational agency does not have knowledge that a child is a child with a disability (in accordance with subparagraph (B)) prior to taking disciplinary measures against the child, the child may be subjected to the same disciplinary measures as measures applied to children without disabilities who engaged in comparable behaviors consistent with clause (ii).

(ii) Limitations. If a request is made for an evaluation of a child during the time period in which the child is subjected to disciplinary measures under paragraph (1) or (2), the evaluation shall be conducted in an expedited manner. If the child is determined to be a child with a disability, taking into consideration information from the evaluation conducted by the agency and information provided by the parents, the agency shall provide special education and related services in accordance with the provisions of this part, except that, pending the results of the evaluation, the child shall remain in the educational placement determined by school authorities.

(m) Transfer of Parental Rights at Age of Majority.

(1) In General. A State that receives amounts from a grant under this part may provide that, when a child with a disability reaches the age of majority under State law (except for a child with a disability who has been determined to be incompetent under State law)—

(A) the public agency shall provide any notice required by this section to both the individual and the parents;

(B) all other rights accorded to parents under this part transfer to the child;

(C) the agency shall notify the individual and the parents of the transfer of rights; and

(D) all rights accorded to parents under this part transfer to children who are incarcerated in an adult or juvenile Federal, State, or local correctional institution.

(2) Special Rule. If, under State law, a child with a disability who has reached the age of majority under State law, who has not been determined to be incompetent, but who is determined not to have the ability to provide informed consent with respect to the educational program of the child, the State shall establish procedures for appointing the parent of the child, or if the parent is not available, another appropriate individual, to represent the educational interests of the child throughout the period of eligibility of the child under this part.

SUBCHAPTER III—INFANT'S AND TODDLERS WITH DISABILITIES

Section 1431. Findings and Policy.

(a) Findings.

The Congress finds that there is an urgent and substantial need —

(1) to enhance the development of infants and toddlers with disabilities and to minimize their potential for developmental delay;

(2) to reduce the educational costs to our society, including our Nation's schools, by minimizing the need for special education and related services after infants and toddlers with disabilities reach school age;

(3) to minimize the likelihood of institutionalization of individuals with disabilities and maximize the potential for their independently living in society;

(4) to enhance the capacity of families to meet the special needs of their infants and toddlers with disabilities; and

(5) to enhance the capacity of State and local agencies and service providers to identify, evaluate, and meet the needs of historically under-represented populations, particularly minority, low-income, inner-city, and rural populations.

(b) Policy.

It is therefore the policy of the United States to provide financial assistance to States—

(1) to develop and implement a statewide, comprehensive, coordinated, multidisciplinary, interagency system that provides early intervention services for infants and toddlers with disabilities and their families;

(2) to facilitate the coordination of payment for early intervention services from Federal, State, local, and private sources (including public and private insurance coverage);

(3) to enhance their capacity to provide quality early intervention services and expand and improve existing early intervention services being provided to infants and toddlers with disabilities and their families; and

(4) to encourage States to expand opportunities for children under 3 years of age who would be at risk of having substantial developmental delay if they did not receive early intervention services.

Section 1436. Individualized Family Service Plan.

(a) Assessment and Program Development.

A statewide system described in Section 1433 shall provide, at a minimum, for each infant or toddler with a disability, and the infant's or toddler's family, to receive —

(1) a multidisciplinary assessment of the unique strengths and needs of the infant or toddler and the identification of services appropriate to meet such needs;

(2) a family-directed assessment of the resources, priorities, and concerns of the family and the identification of the supports and services necessary to enhance the family's capacity to meet the developmental needs of the infant or toddler; and

(3) a written individualized family service plan developed by a multidisciplinary team, including the parents, as required by subsection (e).

(b) Periodic Review.

The individualized family service plan shall be evaluated once a year and the family shall be provided a review of the plan at 6-month intervals (or more often where appropriate based on infant or toddler and family needs).

(c) Promptness After Assessment.

The individualized family service plan shall be developed within a reasonable time after the assessment required by subsection (a)(1) is completed. With the parents' consent, early intervention services may commence prior to the completion of the assessment.

(d) Content of Plan.

The individualized family service plan shall be in writing and contain—

(1) a statement of the infant's or toddler's present levels of physical development, cognitive development, communication development, social or emotional development, and adaptive development, based on objective criteria;

(2) a statement of the family's resources, priorities, and concerns relating to enhancing the development of the family's infant or toddler with a disability;

(3) a statement of the major outcomes expected to be achieved for the infant or toddler and the family, and the criteria, procedures, and timelines used to determine the degree to which progress toward

achieving the outcomes is being made and whether modifications or revisions of the outcomes or services are necessary;

(4) a statement of specific early intervention services necessary to meet the unique needs of the infant or toddler and the family, including the frequency, intensity, and method of delivering services;

(5) a statement of the natural environments in which early intervention services shall appropriately be provided, including a justification of the extent, if any, to which the services will not be provided in a natural environment;

(6) the projected dates for initiation of services and the anticipated duration of the services;

(7) the identification of the service coordinator from the profession most immediately relevant to the infant's or toddler's or family's needs (or who is otherwise qualified to carry out all applicable responsibilities under this part) who will be responsible for the implementation of the plan and coordination with other agencies and persons; and

(8) the steps to be taken to support the transition of the toddler with a disability to preschool or other appropriate services.

(e) Parental Consent.

The contents of the individualized family service plan shall be fully explained to the parents and informed written consent from the parents shall be obtained prior to the provision of early intervention services described in such plan. If the parents do not provide consent with respect to a particular early intervention service, then the early intervention services to which consent is obtained shall be provided.

Section 1439. Procedural Safeguards.

(a) Minimum Procedures.

The procedural safeguards required to be included in a statewide system under Section 1435(a)(13) shall provide, at a minimum, the following:

(1) The timely administrative resolution of complaints by parents. Any party aggrieved by the findings and decision regarding an administrative complaint shall have the right to bring a civil action with respect to the complaint in any State court of competent jurisdiction or in a district court of the United States without regard to the amount in controversy. In any action brought under this paragraph, the court shall receive the records of the administrative proceedings, shall hear additional evidence at the request of a party, and, basing

its decision on the preponderance of the evidence, shall grant such relief as the court determines is appropriate.

(2) The right to confidentiality of personally identifiable information, including the right of parents to written notice of and written consent to the exchange of such information among agencies consistent with Federal and State law.

(3) The right of the parents to determine whether they, their infant or toddler, or other family members will accept or decline any early intervention service under this part in accordance with State law without jeopardizing other early intervention services under this part.

(4) The opportunity for parents to examine records relating to assessment, screening, eligibility determinations, and the development and implementation of the individualized family service plan.

(5) Procedures to protect the rights of the infant or toddler whenever the parents of the infant or toddler are not known or cannot be found or the infant or toddler is a ward of the State, including the assignment of an individual (who shall not be an employee of the State lead agency, or other State agency, and who shall not be any person, or any employee of a person, providing early intervention services to the infant or toddler or any family member of the infant or toddler) to act as a surrogate for the parents.

(6) Written prior notice to the parents of the infant or toddler with a disability whenever the State agency or service provider proposes to initiate or change or refuses to initiate or change the identification, evaluation, or placement of the infant or toddler with a disability, or the provision of appropriate early intervention services to the infant or toddler.

(7) Procedures designed to ensure that the notice required by paragraph (6) fully informs the parents, in the parents' native language, unless it clearly is not feasible to do so, of all procedures available pursuant to this section.

(8) The right of parents to use mediation in accordance with Section 1415(e), except that—

(A) any reference in the section to a State educational agency shall be considered to be a reference to a State's lead agency established or designated under Section 1435(a)(10);

(B) any reference in the section to a local educational agency shall be considered to be a reference to a local service provider or the State's lead agency under this part, as the case may be; and

INDIVIDUALS WITH DISABILITIES EDUCATION ACT

(C) any reference in the section to the provision of free appropriate public education to children with disabilities shall be considered to be a reference to the provision of appropriate early intervention services to infants and toddlers with disabilities.

(b) Services During Pendency of Proceedings.

During the pendency of any proceeding or action involving a complaint by the parents of an infant or toddler with a disability, unless the State agency and the parents otherwise agree, the infant or toddler shall continue to receive the appropriate early intervention services currently being provided or, if applying for initial services, shall receive the services not in dispute.

Section 1482. Parent Training and Information Centers.

(a) Program Authorized.

The Secretary may make grants to, and enter into contracts and cooperative agreements with, parent organizations to support parent training and information centers to carry out activities under this section.

(b) Required Activities.

Each parent training and information center that receives assistance under this section shall—

(1) provide training and information that meets the training and information needs of parents of children with disabilities living in the area served by the center, particularly under-served parents and parents of children who may be inappropriately identified;

(2) assist parents to understand the availability of, and how to effectively use, procedural safeguards under this Act, including encouraging the use, and explaining the benefits, of alternative methods of dispute resolution, such as the mediation process described in Section 1415(e);

(3) serve the parents of infants, toddlers, and children with the full range of disabilities;

(4) assist parents to—

(A) better understand the nature of their children's disabilities and their educational and developmental needs;

(B) communicate effectively with personnel responsible for providing special education, early intervention, and related services;

(C) participate in decision-making processes and the development of individualized education programs under part B and individualized family service plans under part C;

(D) obtain appropriate information about the range of options, programs, services, and resources available to assist children with disabilities and their families;

(E) understand the provisions of this Act for the education of, and the provision of early intervention services to, children with disabilities; and

(F) participate in school reform activities;

(5) in States where the State elects to contract with the parent training and information center, contract with State educational agencies to provide, consistent with subparagraphs (B) and (D) of Section 1415(e)(2), individuals who meet with parents to explain the mediation process to them;

(6) network with appropriate clearinghouses, including organizations conducting national dissemination activities under Section 1485(d), and with other national, State, and local organizations and agencies, such as protection and advocacy agencies, that serve parents and families of children with the full range of disabilities; and

(7) annually report to the Secretary on—

(A) the number of parents to whom it provided information and training in the most recently concluded fiscal year; and

(B) the effectiveness of strategies used to reach and serve parents, including under-served parents of children with disabilities.

(c) Optional Activities.

A parent training and information center that receives assistance under this section may—

(1) provide information to teachers and other professionals who provide special education and related services to children with disabilities;

(2) assist students with disabilities to understand their rights and responsibilities under Section 1415(m) on reaching the age of majority; and

(3) assist parents of children with disabilities to be informed participants in the development and implementation of the State's State improvement plan under subpart 1.

(d) Application Requirements.

Each application for assistance under this section shall identify with specificity the special efforts that the applicant will undertake—

(1) to ensure that the needs for training and information of under-served parents of children with disabilities in the area to be served are effectively met; and

(2) to work with community-based organizations.

(e) Distribution of Funds.

(1) In General. The Secretary shall make at least 1 award to a parent organization in each State, unless the Secretary does not receive an application from such an organization in each State of sufficient quality to warrant approval.

(2) Selection Requirement. The Secretary shall select among applications submitted by parent organizations in a State in a manner that ensures the most effective assistance to parents, including parents in urban and rural areas, in the State.

(f) Quarterly Review.

(1) Requirements.

(A) Meetings. The board of directors or special governing committee of each organization that receives an award under this section shall meet at least once in each calendar quarter to review the activities for which the award was made.

(B) Advising Board. Each special governing committee shall directly advise the organization's governing board of its views and recommendations.

(2) Continuation Award. When an organization requests a continuation award under this section, the board of directors or special governing committee shall submit to the Secretary a written review of the parent training and information program conducted by the organization during the preceding fiscal year.

(g) Definition of Parent Organization.

As used in this section, the term parent organization' means a private nonprofit organization (other than an institution of higher education) that—

(1) has a board of directors—

(A) the majority of whom are parents of children with disabilities;

(B) that includes—

(i) individuals working in the fields of special education, related services, and early intervention; and

(ii) individuals with disabilities; and

(C) the parent and professional members of which are broadly representative of the population to be served; or

(2) has—

(A) a membership that represents the interests of individuals with disabilities and has established a special governing committee that meets the requirements of paragraph (1); and

(B) a memorandum of understanding between the special governing committee and the board of directors of the organization that clearly outlines the relationship between the board and the committee and the decision-making responsibilities and authority of each.

Section 1483. Community Parent Resource Centers.

(a) In General.

The Secretary may make grants to, and enter into contracts and cooperative agreements with, local parent organizations to support parent training and information centers that will help ensure that under-served parents of children with disabilities, including low-income parents, parents of children with limited English proficiency, and parents with disabilities, have the training and information they need to enable them to participate effectively in helping their children with disabilities—

(1) to meet developmental goals and, to the maximum extent possible, those challenging standards that have been established for all children; and

(2) to be prepared to lead productive independent adult lives, to the maximum extent possible.

(b) Required Activities.

Each parent training and information center assisted under this section shall—

(1) provide training and information that meets the training and information needs of parents of children with disabilities proposed to be served by the grant, contract, or cooperative agreement;

(2) carry out the activities required of parent training and information centers under paragraphs (2) through (7) of Section 1482(b);

(3) establish cooperative partnerships with the parent training and information centers funded under Section 1482; and

(4) be designed to meet the specific needs of families who experience significant isolation from available sources of information and support.

(c) Definition.

As used is this section, the term 'local parent organization' means a parent organization, as defined in Section 1482(g), that either—

(1) has a board of directors the majority of whom are from the community to be served; or

(2) has—

(A) as a part of its mission, serving the interests of individuals with disabilities from such community; and

(B) a special governing committee to administer the grant, contract, or cooperative agreement, a majority of the members of which are individuals from such community.

Section 1484. Technical Assistance for Parent Training and Information Centers.

(a) In General.

The Secretary may, directly or through awards to eligible entities, provide technical assistance for developing, assisting, and coordinating parent training and information programs carried out by parent training and information centers receiving assistance under sections 1482 and 1483.

(b) Authorized Activities.

The Secretary may provide technical assistance to a parent training and information center under this section in areas such as—

(1) effective coordination of parent training efforts;

(2) dissemination of information;

(3) evaluation by the center of itself;

(4) promotion of the use of technology, including assistive technology devices and assistive technology services;

(5) reaching under-served populations;

(6) including children with disabilities in general education programs;

(7) facilitation of transitions from—
- (A) early intervention services to preschool;
- (B) preschool to school; and
- (C) secondary school to post-secondary environments; and

(8) promotion of alternative methods of dispute resolution.

APPENDIX 13: SELECTED PROVISIONS OF THE AMERICANS WITH DISABILITIES ACT OF 1990

TITLE II—PUBLIC SERVICES

Subtitle A. Prohibition Against Discrimination and Other Generally Applicable Provisions

Section 12131. Definitions

As used in this subchapter:

(1) Public entity—The term "public entity" means—

(A) any State or local government;

(B) any department, agency, special purpose district, or other instrumentality of a State or States or local government; and

(C) the National Railroad Passenger Corporation, and any commuter authority (as defined in section 24102(4) of title 49).

(2) Qualified individual with a disability—The term "qualified individual with a disability" means an individual with a disability who, with or without reasonable modifications to rules, policies, or practices, the removal of architectural, communication, or transportation barriers, or the provision of auxiliary aids and services, meets the essential eligibility requirements for the receipt of services or the participation in programs or activities provided by a public entity.

Section 12132. Discrimination

Subject to the provisions of this subchapter, no qualified individual with a disability shall, by reason of such disability, be excluded from participation in or be denied the benefits of the services, programs, or activities of a public entity, or be subjected to discrimination by any such entity.

SELECTED PROVISIONS OF THE AMERICANS WITH DISABILITIES ACT OF 1990

Section 12133. Enforcement

The remedies, procedures, and rights set forth in section 794a of title 29 shall be the remedies, procedures, and rights this subchapter provides to any person alleging discrimination on the basis of disability in violation of section 12132 of this title.

Section 12134. Regulations

(a) In general

Not later than 1 year after July 26, 1990, the Attorney General shall promulgate regulations in an accessible format that implement this part. Such regulations shall not include any matter within the scope of the authority of the Secretary of Transportation under section 12143, 12149, or 12164 of this title.

(b) Relationship to other regulations

Except for "program accessibility, existing facilities", and "communications", regulations under subsection (a) of this section shall be consistent with this chapter and with the coordination regulations under part 41 of title 28, Code of Federal Regulations (as promulgated by the Department of Health, Education, and Welfare on January 13, 1978), applicable to recipients of Federal financial assistance under section 794 of title 29. With respect to "program accessibility, existing facilities", and "communications", such regulations shall be consistent with regulations and analysis as in part 39 of title 28 of the Code of Federal Regulations, applicable to federally conducted activities under section 794 of title 29.

(c) Standards

Regulations under subsection (a) of this section shall include standards applicable to facilities and vehicles covered by this part, other than facilities, stations, rail passenger cars, and vehicles covered by part B of this subchapter. Such standards shall be consistent with the minimum guidelines and requirements issued by the Architectural and Transportation Barriers Compliance Board in accordance with section 12204(a) of this title.

SECTION 502. STATE IMMUNITY

A State shall not be immune under the eleventh amendment to the Constitution of the United States from an action in Federal or State court of competent jurisdiction for a violation of this Act. In any action against a State for a violation of the requirements of this Act, remedies (including remedies both at law and in equity) are available for such a violation to the same extent as such remedies are available for such a violation in an action against any public or private entity other than a State.

SECTION 503. PROHIBITION AGAINST RETALIATION AND COERCION

(a) Retaliation. No person shall discriminate against any individual because such individual has opposed any act or practice made unlawful by this Act or because such individual made a charge, testified, assisted, or participated in any manner in an investigation, proceeding, or hearing under this Act.

(b) Interference, Coercion, or Intimidation. It shall be unlawful to coerce, intimidate, threaten, or interfere with any individual in the exercise or enjoyment of, or on account of his or her having exercised or enjoyed, or on account of his or her having aided or encouraged any other individual in the exercise or enjoyment of, any right granted or protected by this Act.

(c) Remedies and Procedures. The remedies and procedures available under sections 107, 203, and 308 of this Act shall be available to aggrieved persons for violations of subsections (a) and (b), with respect to title I, title II and title III, respectively.

SECTION 505. ATTORNEYS FEES

In any action or administrative proceeding commenced pursuant to this Act, the court or agency, in its discretion, may allow the prevailing party, other than the United States, a reasonable attorneys fee, including litigation expenses, and costs, and the United States shall be liable for the foregoing the same as a private individual.

APPENDIX 14: TRANSITIONING RESOURCE DIRECTORY

ORGANIZATION	WEBSITE	MISSION
A Call to Parents	www.calltoparents.org/info.html	website provides resources to help parent's guide their youth through high school to college by assisting their youth in determining their natural talents, identify the appropriate training, and explore all educational options
Adolescent Health Transition Project	http://depts.washington.edu/healthtr/Teens	website contains information, materials, and links to others with an interest in health transition issues
Age of Majority: Preparing Your Child for Making Good Choices (Parent Brief May 2002)	www.ncset.org/publications	A parent brief from the National Center for Secondary Education and Transition (NCSET) provides information for parents to help their child prepare for the age of majority
Americans with Disabilities Act-A Guide for People with Disabilities Seeking Employment	www.ssa.gov/work/	website provides information on the Americans with Disabilities Act and its applications for people with disabilities who are seeking employment

TRANSITIONING RESOURCE DIRECTORY

ORGANIZATION	WEBSITE	MISSION
America's CareerInfoNet	www.acinet.org	website provides information people need to make smart career choices and find the training they need to implement that choice
America's Teens.Gov	www.afterschool.gov/kidsnteens2.html	website provides an internet information center for teenagers, information about college and finding a job, learning opportunities, and a discussion of issues that concern teenagers
Career Key	www.careerkey.org/english/	Career Key helps identify jobs and learn about salary job outlook and job training requirements
CareersNet.Org	www.careersnet.org/TAEC/job_shadows.htm	website provides a sample job shadow student checklist, student questionnaire, student evaluation, and a job shadow grading criteria sheet.
Center for Self-Determination	www.self-determination.com/publications/community2.html	none listed
Decision Making/Problem Solving with Teens	http://ohioline.osu.edu/flm98/pdf/fs05.pdf	A fact sheet listing and explaining nine ways in which parents can help their teenagers make important decisions
Employer Expectations	www.csun.edu/~sp20558/dis/about.html	website provides information about building work relationships and discusses first career experiences
Family Village	www.familyvillage.wisc.edu/	website contains a global community of disability-related resources

ORGANIZATION	WEBSITE	MISSION
DO-IT (Disabilities Opportunities Internetworking and Technology) Center	www.washington.edu/doit/Brochures/Parents/naparent.htm	website provides national resources for parents of children with disabilities including organizations that promote self advocacy, assistive technology, and transition planning
Full Life Ahead: A Workbook and Guide to Adult Life for Students and Families of Students with Disabilities	www.fulllifeahead.org/	a guide to help families successfully work through the transition process
Health Care Transition for Youth Digest	http://mchenet.ichp.edu/scripts/	website contains information for youth and young adults with special health care needs, their families, and professionals with whom they interact
JobBankUSA	www.jobbankusa.com	website offers online information about careers
National Center on Secondary Education and Transition	http://ici.umn.edu/ncset/publications/parent	none listed
National Mentoring Partnership	www.mentoring.org	website contains information about mentoring: how to find one, become one, and ideas for activities
Positive Parenting of Teens Adolescents and Decision Making	www.extension.umn.edu/distribution/familydevelopment/	provides information for parents about fostering youth decision making skills
Ten Steps to Mapping Your Future: Middle and High School Students	www.mapping-your-future.org/	Mapping Your Future is a free service that provides information on topics relevant for higher education and career planning.

TRANSITIONING RESOURCE DIRECTORY

ORGANIZATION	WEBSITE	MISSION
To Tell or Not to Tell: Disclosure...That is the Question	www.udel.edu/CSC/disclosure.html	website gives information to help an employee decide to disclose a disability and answers common questions one may have about disclosing a disability
TransitionLink	www.transitionlink.com/	provides tips for parents on starting the transition planning process as early as elementary school and how to continue the transition planning through high school
VolunteerMatch	www.volunteermatch.org/	this website provides leads for those seeking volunteer opportunities by a searchable database
Work-Based Learning and Future Employment for Youth: A Guide for Parents and Guardians	http://ncset.org/publications/	publication from the National Center for Secondary Education and Transition (NCSET) which discusses how work-based learning can help youth develop important skills, and strategies for successfully participating in a work-based learning program
Youth Build	www.youthbuild.org/	website contains information about Youth Build programs and how to participate
Youth Rules!	www.youthrules.dol.gov	Department of Labor website which provides information on how youth, parents, educators, and employers can participate in youth workforce development

APPENDIX 15:
TABLE OF TICKETS ISSUED UNDER THE TICKET TO WORK PROGRAM AS OF MAY 2005, BY STATE

STATE	TICKETS ISSUED
ALABAMA	244,028
ALASKA	16,680
ARIZONA	193,498
ARKANSAS	156,633
CALIFORNIA	1,012,042
COLORADO	114,337
CONNECTICUT	105,133
DISTRICT OF COLUMBIA	23,236
DELAWARE	31,074
FLORIDA	655,562
GEORGIA	323,825
HAWAII	30,717
IDAHO	40,792
ILLINOIS	430,400
INDIANA	216,498
IOWA	96,488
KANSAS	80,747
KENTUCKY	280,969
LOUSIANA	227,816
MARYLAND	142,188
MAINE	63,588
MASSACHUSETTS	264,754
MICHIGAN	400,659

TICKETS ISSUED UNDER THE TICKET TO WORK PROGRAM

STATE	TICKETS ISSUED
MINNESOTA	131,999
MISSISSIPPI	179,763
MISSOURI	242,867
MONTANA	31,729
NEBRASKA	45,754
NEVADA	66,221
NEW HAMPSHIRE	42,161
NEW JERSEY	246,769
NEW MEXICO	74,723
NEW YORK	794,494
NORTH CAROLINA	342,250
NORTH DAKOTA	16,835
OHIO	404,196
OKLAHOMA	152,216
OREGON	122,719
PENNSYLVANIA	476,600
RHODE ISLAND	43,672
SOUTH CAROLINA	207,552
SOUTH DAKOTA	22,762
TENNESSEE	288,348
TEXAS	589,994
UTAH	41,382
VERMONT	25,271
VIRGINIA	252,695
WASHINGTON	188,285
WEST VIRGINIA	131,393
WISCONSIN	182,151
WYOMING	13,088

GLOSSARY

Accommodation—A term used in the context of public accommodations and facilities that an individual with a disability may not be excluded, denied services, segregated or otherwise treated differently than other individuals by a public accommodation or commercial facility.

Achievement levels—Achievement levels define what students should know and be able to do at different levels of performance as follows: (1) Basic level denotes partial mastery of prerequisite knowledge and skills that are fundamental for proficient work at each grade; (2) Proficient level represents solid academic performance for each grade assessed, and competency over challenging subject matter, including subject-matter knowledge, application of such knowledge to real-world situations, and analytical skills appropriate to the subject matter; (3) Advanced level signifies superior performance.

Action at Law—A judicial proceeding whereby one party prosecutes another for a wrong done.

Actual Damages—Actual damages are those damages directly referable to the breach or tortious act, and which can be readily proven to have been sustained, and for which the injured party should be compensated as a matter of right.

Alternative Keyboard—Alternative keyboards may be different from standard keyboards in size, shape, layout, or function. They offer individuals with special needs greater efficiency, control, and comfort.

Alternative Schools—Alternative schools serve students whose needs cannot be met in a regular, special education, or vocational school, e.g., schools for potential dropouts; residential treatment centers for substance abuse; schools for chronic truants; and schools for students with behavioral problems.

GLOSSARY

Ambulation Aids—Devices that help people walk upright, including canes, crutches, and walkers.

American Civil Liberties Union (ACLU)—A nationwide organization dedicated to the enforcement and preservation of rights and civil liberties guaranteed by the federal and state constitutions.

Americans with Disabilities Act (ADA)—A federal law which prohibits discrimination on the basis of a "qualified" disability as set forth in the statute.

Americans with Disability Act Accessibility Guidelines (ADAAG)—Technical standard for accessible design of new construction or alterations adopted by the Department of Justice for places of public accommodation pursuant to Title III of the ADA.

A Nation at Risk—A report published by the U.S. Department of Education in highlighting deficiencies in knowledge of the nation's students and population as a whole in areas such as literacy, mathematics, geography, and basic science.

Appropriations—Budget authority provided through the congressional appropriation process that permits federal agencies to incur obligations and to make payments.

Architectural Barrier—A physical feature of a public accommodation that limits or prevents disabled persons from obtaining the goods or services offered.

Assistive Technology Device—Any item, piece of equipment, or product system, whether acquired commercially off the shelf, modified, or customized, that is used to increase, maintain, or improve functional capabilities of a child with a disability.

Assistive Technology Service—Any service that directly assists a child with a disability in the selection, acquisition, or use of an assistive technology device.

At-risk—Being "at-risk" means having one or more family background or other risk factors that have been found to predict a high rate of school failure—e.g., retention or dropping out—at some time in the future, including having a mother whose education is less than high school, living in a single-parent family, receiving welfare assistance, and living in a household where the primary language spoken is other than English.

Augmentative Communication System—Any system that increases or improves communication of individuals with receptive or expressive communication impairments. The system can include speech, gestures, sign language, symbols, synthesized speech, dedicated communication devices, microcomputers, and other communication systems.

Braille—A raised dot printed language that is used by persons with visual impairments. Each raised dot configuration represents a letter or word combination.

Braille Embossers and Translators—A Braille embosser transfers computer-generated text into embossed braille output. Translation programs convert text scanned in or generated via standard word processing programs into Braille that can be printed on the embosser.

Burden of Proof—The duty of a party to substantiate an allegation or issue to convince the trier of fact as to the truth of their claim.

Capacity—Capacity is the legal qualification concerning the ability of one to understand the nature and effects of one's acts.

Captioning—A text transcript of the audio portion of multimedia products, such as video and television, that is synchronized to the visual events taking place on screen.

Child Abuse—Any form of cruelty to a child's physical, moral or mental well-being.

Child Protective Agency—A state agency responsible for the investigation of child abuse and neglect reports.

Child Welfare—A generic term which embraces the totality of measures necessary for a child's well being; physical, moral and mental.

Child Aged 3 Through 9—The term "child with a disability" for a child aged 3 through 9 may, at the discretion of the State and the local educational agency, include a child: (i) experiencing developmental delays, as defined by the State and as measured by appropriate diagnostic instruments and procedures, in one or more of the following areas: physical development, cognitive development, communication development, social or emotional development, or adaptive development; and (ii) who, by reason thereof, needs special education and related services.

Child With a Disability—In general, refers to a child: (i) with mental retardation, hearing impairments including deafness, speech or language impairments, visual impairments including blindness, serious emotional disturbance, orthopedic impairments, autism, traumatic brain injury, other health impairments, or specific learning disabilities; and (ii) who, by reason thereof, needs special education and related services.

Circumstantial Evidence—Indirect evidence by which a principal fact may be inferred.

GLOSSARY

Compensatory Revenue—A type of categorical revenue that targets resources to school districts for instruction and other supplemental services for educationally disadvantaged students.

Constitution—The fundamental principles of law which frame a governmental system.

Constitutional Right—Refers to the individual liberties granted by the constitution of a state or the federal government.

Corporal Punishment—Physical punishment as distinguished from pecuniary punishment or a fine; any kind of punishment of, or inflicted on, the body.

Court—The branch of government responsible for the resolution of disputes arising under the laws of the government.

Damages—In general, damages refers to monetary compensation which the law awards to one who has been injured by the actions of another, such as in the case of tortious conduct or breach of contractual obligations.

Delinquent—An infant of not more than a specified age who has violated criminal laws or has engaged in disobedient, indecent or immoral conduct, and is in need of treatment, rehabilitation, or supervision.

Disability—Under the ADA, an individual is considered disabled if he or she (i) is substantially impaired with respect to a major life activity; (ii) has a record of such an impairment; or (iii) is regarded as having an impairment.

Digitized Speech—Human speech that is recorded onto an integrated circuit chip and which has the ability to be played back.

Display—Assistive technology that raises or lowers dot patterns based on input from an electronic device such as a screen reader or text browser.

Due Process Rights—All rights which are of such fundamental importance as to require compliance with due process standards of fairness and justice.

Duty—The obligation, to which the law will give recognition and effect, to conform to a particular standard of conduct toward another.

Educational Attainment—The highest level of schooling attended and completed.

Educational Service Agency—Refers to (A) a regional public multi-service agency: (i) authorized by State law to develop, manage, and provide services or programs to local educational agencies; and

(ii) recognized as an administrative agency for purposes of the provision of special education and related services provided within public elementary and secondary schools of the State; and (B) includes any other public institution or agency having administrative control and direction over a public elementary or secondary school.

Electronic Pointing Devices—Electronic pointing devices allow the user to control the cursor on the screen using ultrasound, an infrared beam, eye movements, nerve signals, or brains waves. When used with an on-screen keyboard, electronic pointing devices also allow the user to enter text or data.

Elementary School—A nonprofit institutional day or residential school that provides elementary education, as determined under state law.

English as a Second Language (ESL)—Programs that provide intensive instruction in English for students with limited English proficiency.

Enrollment—The total number of students registered in a given school unit at a given time, generally in the fall of a year.

Environmental Control Unit (ECU)—A system that enables individuals to control various electronic devices in their environment through a variety of alternative access methods, such as switch or voice access. Target devices include lights, televisions, telephones, music players, door openers, security systems, and kitchen appliances. Also referred to as Electronic Aid to Daily Living (EADL).

Equal access—Equal opportunity of a qualified person with a disability to participate in or benefit from educational aids, benefits, or services.

Equipment—The term "equipment" includes (A) machinery, utilities, and built-in equipment and any necessary enclosures or structures to house such machinery, utilities, or equipment; and (B) all other items necessary for the functioning of a particular facility as a facility for the provision of educational services, including items such as instructional equipment and necessary furniture; printed, published, and audio-visual instructional materials; telecommunications, sensory, and other technological aids and devices; and books, periodicals, documents, and other related materials.

Excess Costs—Those costs that are in excess of the average annual per-student expenditure in a local educational agency during the preceding school year for an elementary or secondary school student, as may be appropriate, and which shall be computed after deducting (A)

GLOSSARY

amounts received: (i) under part B of this title; (ii) under part A of title I of the Elementary and Secondary Education Act of 1965; or (iii) under part A of title VII of that Act; and (B) any State or local funds expended for programs that would qualify for assistance under any of those parts.

Free Appropriate Public Education—A term used in the elementary and secondary school context; refers to the provision of regular or special education and related aids and services that are designed to meet individual educational needs of students with disabilities as adequately as the needs of students without disabilities are met and is based upon adherence to procedures that satisfy the Section 504 requirements pertaining to educational setting, evaluation and placement, and procedural safeguards.

Guardian—A person who is entrusted with the management of the property and/or person of another who is incapable, due to age or incapacity, to administer their own affairs.

Hearing Impairment—An impairment in hearing, whether permanent or fluctuating, that adversely affects a child's educational performance, in the most severe case, because the child is impaired in processing linguistic information through hearing.

High school—A secondary school offering the final years of high school work necessary for graduation.

Indian—An individual who is a member of an Indian tribe.

Indian Tribe—Any Federal or State Indian tribe, band, rancheria, pueblo, colony, or community, including any Alaskan Native village or regional village corporation (as defined in or established under the Alaska Native Claims Settlement Act).

Individualized Education Program (IEP)—A written statement for each child with a disability that is developed, reviewed, and revised in accordance with section 1414(d).

Individuals with Disabilities Education Act (IDEA)—A statute requiring public schools to provide a free public education to disabled children in the least restrictive environment appropriate for the child's needs.

In Loco Parentis—Latin for "in the place of a parent." Refers to an individual who assumes parental obligations and status without a formal, legal adoption.

Infancy—The period prior to reaching the legal age of majority.

Judge—The individual who presides over a court, and whose function it is to determine controversies.

Keyguards—Keyguards are hard plastic covers with holes for each key. Using a keyguard, someone with an unsteady finger or with a pointing device can avoid striking unwanted keys.

Local Educational Agency—A public board of education or other public authority legally constituted within a State for either administrative control or direction of, or to perform a service function for, public elementary or secondary schools in a city, county, township, school district, or other political subdivision of a State, or for such combination of school districts or counties as are recognized in a State as an administrative agency for its public elementary or secondary schools.

Minor—A person who has not yet reached the age of majority.

Modal Grade—The modal grade is the year of school in which the largest proportion of students of a given age are enrolled and classified according to their relative progress in school, i.e., whether the grade or year in which they were enrolled was below, at, or above the modal or typical grade for persons of their age at the time of the survey.

Multiple disabilities—Concomitant impairments—e.g., mental retardation-blindness, mental retardation-orthopedic impairment, etc.—the combination of which causes such severe educational problems that they cannot be accommodated in special education programs solely for one of the impairments. The term does not include deaf-blindness.

Native Language—With reference to an individual of limited English proficiency, means the language normally used by the individual, or in the case of a child, the language normally used by the parents of the child.

Nonprofit—With reference to a school, agency, organization, or institution, means a school, agency, organization, or institution owned and operated by one or more nonprofit corporations or associations no part of the net earnings of which inures, or may lawfully inure, to the benefit of any private shareholder or individual.

Occupational Education—Refers to vocational education programs that prepare students for a specific occupation or cluster of occupations, including agriculture, business, marketing, health care, protective services, trade and industrial, technology, food service, child care, and personal and other services programs.

Onscreen Keyboard—On-screen keyboards are software images of a standard or modified keyboard placed on the computer screen by soft-

GLOSSARY

ware. The keys are selected by a mouse, touch screen, trackball, joystick, switch, or electronic pointing device.

Optical Character Recognition and Scanners—Optical character recognition (OCR) software works with a scanner to convert images from a printed page into a standard computer file. A scanner is a device that converts an image from a printed page to a computer file. With optical character recognition software, the resulting computer file can be edited.

Orthopedic Impairments—Refers to a severe orthopedic impairment that adversely affects a child's educational performance, including impairments caused by congenital anomaly, e.g., clubfoot, absence of some member, etc.; impairments caused by disease, e.g., poliomyelitis, bone tuberculosis, etc.; and impairments from other causes, e.g., cerebral palsy, amputations, and fractures or burns that cause contractures.

Other Support Services Staff—Refers to all staff not reported in other categories, including media personnel, social workers, data processors, health maintenance workers, bus drivers, security, cafeteria workers, and other staff.

Outlying Areas—Includes the United States Virgin Islands, Guam, American Samoa, and the Commonwealth of the Northern Mariana Islands.

Parens Patriae—Latin for "parent of his country." Refers to the role of the state as guardian of legally disabled individuals.

Parent—The term "parent" (A) includes a legal guardian; and (B) except as used in sections 1415(b)(2) and 1439(a)(5), includes an individual assigned under either of those sections to be a surrogate parent.

Placement—A term used in the elementary and secondary school context; refers to a regular and/or special educational program in which a student receives educational and/or related services.

Prima Facie Case—A case which is sufficient on its face, being supported by at least the requisite minimum of evidence, and being free from palpable defects.

Reading literacy—Reading literacy is defined as understanding, using, and reflecting on written texts in order to achieve one's goals, to develop one's knowledge and potential, and to participate in society.

Reasonable accommodation—A term used in the employment context to refer to modifications or adjustments employers make to a job application process, the work environment, the manner or circumstances under which the position held or desired is customarily performed, or that enable a covered entity's employee with a disability to enjoy equal benefits and privileges of employment.

Regular School Districts—A regular school district can be either: (1) a school district that is not a component of a supervisory union; or (2) a school district component of a supervisory union that shares a superintendent and administrative services with other local school districts.

Regular schools—Schools that are part of state and local school systems as well as private elementary/secondary schools, both religiously affiliated and nonsectarian, that are not alternative schools, vocational education schools, special education schools, subcollegiate departments of postsecondary institutions, residential schools for exceptional children, federal schools for American Indians or Alaska Natives, or federal schools on military posts and other federal installations.

Rehabilitation Act of 1973—A disability discrimination statute which preceded and served as a model for the ADA.

Related Services—Refers to transportation, and such developmental, corrective, and other supportive services, including speech-language pathology and audiology services, psychological services, physical and occupational therapy, recreation, including therapeutic recreation, social work services, counseling services, including rehabilitation counseling, orientation and mobility services, and medical services, except that such medical services shall be for diagnostic and evaluation purposes only as may be required to assist a child with a disability to benefit from special education, and includes the early identification and assessment of disabling conditions in children.

Remedial Education—Instruction for a student lacking the reading, writing, mathematics, or other skills necessary to perform college-level work at the level required by the attended institution.

Scale score—Uses a set scale to assess overall achievement in a domain, such as mathematics.

School District—Also referred to as a local education agency (LEA), refers to an education agency at the local level that exists primarily to operate public schools or to contract for public school services.

Screen Enlargement Programs—Screen enlargement programs magnify a portion of the screen, increasing the visibility for some users with limited vision. Most have variable magnification levels. Some screen enlargement programs offer text-to-speech.

GLOSSARY

Screen Reader—A screen reader is a software program that uses synthesized speech to "speak" graphics and text out loud. This type of program is used by people with limited vision or blindness.

Seating and Positioning Aids—Modifications to wheelchairs or other seating systems that provide greater body stability, upright posture or reduction of pressure on the skin surface.

Secondary School—A nonprofit institutional day or residential school that provides secondary education, as determined under State law, except that it does not include any education beyond grade 12.

Secretary—The term "Secretary" as used herein refers to the Secretary of Education.

Service Animal—Refers to an animal, such as a guide dog, which has been trained to provide assistance to disabled individuals.

Special education schools—Special education schools provide educational services to students with special physical or mental needs—i.e., students with mental disabilities (such as mental retardation or autism); physical disabilities (such as hearing impairments); or learning disabilities (such as dyslexia).

Specific learning disabilities—A disorder in one or more of the basic psychological processes involved in understanding or in using language, spoken or written, that may manifest itself in an imperfect ability to listen, think, speak, read, write, spell, or do mathematical calculations, including such conditions as perceptual disabilities, brain injury, minimal brain dysfunction, dyslexia, and developmental aphasia. The term does not apply to children who have learning problems that are primarily the result of visual, hearing, or motor disabilities; of mental retardation; of emotional disturbance; or of environmental, cultural, or economic disadvantage.

Speech or language impairments—A communication disorder such as stuttering, impaired articulation, a language impairment, or a voice impairment that adversely affects a child's educational performance.

Standing—The legal right of an individual or group to use the courts to resolve an existing controversy.

State—Refers to each of the 50 States, the District of Columbia, the Commonwealth of Puerto Rico, and each of the outlying areas.

State Educational Agency—The State board of education or other agency or officer primarily responsible for the State supervision of public elementary and secondary schools, or, if there is no such officer or agency, an officer or agency designated by the Governor or by State law.

GLOSSARY

Status Offender—A child who commits an act which is not criminal in nature, but which nevertheless requires some sort of intervention and disciplinary attention merely because of the age of the offender.

Statute of Limitations—Any law which fixes the time within which parties must take judicial action to enforce rights or thereafter be barred from enforcing them.

Supplementary Aids and Services—Refers to aids, services, and other supports that are provided in regular education classes or other education-related settings to enable children with disabilities to be educated with nondisabled children to the maximum extent appropriate under the applicable statute.

Supreme Court—In most jurisdictions, the Supreme Court is the highest appellate court, including the federal court system.

Talking Word Processors—A talking word processor is a software program that uses synthesized speech to provide auditory feedback of what has been typed.

TTD or TTY—A Telecommunication Device for the Deaf (TTY or TDD) is a device with a keyboard that sends and receives typed messages over a telephone line.

Telecommunications Device for the Deaf (TDD)—An auxiliary aid consisting of a keyboard and display which is attached to a telephone and used by individuals with hearing or speech impairments to communicate on the telephone.

Telecommunications Relay Services (TRS)—A service which enables hearing or speech impaired callers to communicate with each other through a third party communications assistant using a TDD.

Traditional Public School—All public schools that are not public charter schools or Bureau of Indian Affairs-funded schools operated by local public school districts, including regular, special education, vocational/technical, and alternative schools.

Transition Services—Refers to a coordinated set of activities for a student with a disability that (A) are designed within an outcome-oriented process, which promotes movement from school to post-school activities, including post-secondary education, vocational training, integrated employment, including supported employment, continuing and adult education, adult services, independent living, or community participation; (B) are based upon the individual student's needs, taking into account the student's preferences and interests; and (C) include instruction, related services, community experiences, the development of employment and other post-school adult living objectives, and, when

GLOSSARY

appropriate, acquisition of daily living skills and functional vocational evaluation.

Truancy—Willful and unjustified failure to attend school by one who is required to attend.

Unconstitutional—Refers to a statute which conflicts with the United States Constitution rendering it void.

Vocational Education Schools—Vocational schools primarily serve students who are being trained for semi-skilled or technical occupations.

Voice Recognition—Voice recognition allows the user to speak to the computer instead of using a keyboard or mouse to input data or control computer functions.

BIBLIOGRAPHY AND ADDITIONAL RESOURCES

The ACLU Department of Public Education (Date Visited: May 2005) <http:www.aclu.org/>

American Academy of Emergency Physicians (Date Visited: May 2005) <http://www.acep.org/>

American Academy of Pediatrics (Date Visited: May 2005 <www.aap. org/>

Black's Law Dictionary, Fifth Edition. St. Paul, MN: West Publishing Company, 1979

Edlaw, Inc. (Date Visited: May 2005) <http://www.edlaw.net/>

The Library of Education (Date Visited: May 2005) <Library@inet.ed. gov>

National Dissemination Center for Children with Disabilities (Date Visited: May 2005) <www.nichcy.org/>

The United States Department of Education (Date Visited: May 2005) <http://www.ed.gov/>

The United States Department of Education Educational Resources Information Center (Date Visited: May 2005) <askeric@ericir.syr.edu/>

The United States Department of Education Office of Special Education and Rehabilitative Services (Date Visited: May 2005) <www.ed.gov/offices/osers/>

The United States Department of Labor (Date Visited: May 2005) <http://www.dol.gov/>.

The United States Equal Opportunity Commission (Date Visited: 2005) <http://www.eeoc.gov/>.

The United States Social Security Administration (Date Visited: May 2005) <http://www.ssa.gov/>.